'If you were going to read just one book on cannabis make it this one. Copeland and colleagues shine a light on the world's favourite and most misunderstood drug—if you think that cannabis is not addictive think again. This book is written in a style that will appeal to any reader whether it's the adolescent cannabis user, the parent, the drug treatment professional, or the addiction expert—all of these will find something new in the authors' accumulated decades of experience.'

Neil McKeganey, *PhD FRSA, Director, Centre for Drug Misuse Research, Glasgow, Scotland.*

'... provides a breath of fresh air and clarity for those trying to make sense of the complex and conflicting dialogue on cannabis (marijuana). . . . a concise, easy to read, scientific, yet common-sense perspective on the world's favorite drug.'

Alan J. Budney, *PhD Professor, Geisel School of Medicine at Dartmouth DH Addiction Treatment and Research Program, New Hampshire, USA.*

Quit Cannabis

An expert guide to coping with cravings and withdrawal, unscrambling your brain and kicking the habit for good

Jan Copeland, Sally Rooke
and Etty Matalon

ALLEN&UNWIN

First published in 2015

Allen & Unwin
83 Alexander Street
Crows Nest NSW 2065
Australia
Phone: (61 2) 8425 0100
Email: info@allenandunwin.com
Web: www.allenandunwin.com

Cataloguing-in-Publication details are available
from the National Library of Australia
www.trove.nla.gov.au

ISBN 978 1 74331 992 5

Set in 11/15 pt EideticNeo by Midland Typesetters, Australia
Printed and bound in Australia by McPherson's Printing Group

10 9 8 7 6 5 4 3 2 1

Contents

About the authors

Jan Copeland is the founding Professor and Director of the National Cannabis Prevention and Information Centre (NCPIC) at the University of New South Wales (UNSW Australia). She has pioneered a range of studies developing brief interventions for cannabis-related problems for adults and adolescents, and has led the development of a program of work that measures and treats cannabis withdrawal with cannabinoid medications and cognitive behavioural treatment. Jan works with a number of community-based agencies on service evaluations and executive management. She is a member of the Australian Psychological Society, the Australian Professional Society on Alcohol and Drugs, the International Cannabinoid Research Society, the International Society for Research on Internet Interventions and the US College on Problems of Drug Dependence, where she serves as the Chair of the college's International Research Committee. She is on the editorial board of a number of international journals and is an Associate Editor of the leading US journal *Drug and Alcohol Dependence*.

Sally Rooke joined NCPIC in September 2008. She has led a range of projects developing and evaluating the effectiveness of a web-based treatment for individuals who wish to reduce their cannabis use, web-based assessments and brief advice, and a smartphone application for cannabis use problems. She completed a PhD in psychology, examining the decision-making processes that lead to adolescent and adult substance use. She has led studies on the effects of graphic warning for tobacco and cannabis, and the characteristics of successful and unsuccessful quitters.

Etty Matalon is a clinical psychologist and the National Clinical Training Manager for the NCPIC. She was the state president of the Australian Association for Cognitive and Behaviour Therapy for five years. She has more than 20 years' clinical experience in the field of alcohol and other drugs in a range of settings. Throughout her career, she has worked closely with the Australian National Drug and Alcohol Research Centre at UNSW Australia and has provided clinical services in relation to several trials and clinical expertise to several publications.

Foreword

A remarkable series of events has occurred in the science and politics of cannabis over the past 30 years.

In an interesting paradox, science has revealed startling things about how cannabis affects the brain, and how it can have an impact on motor skills, memory, lung function, and IQ, yet there is simultaneously a growing public acceptance of the drug. It's a strange asymmetry that can be explained partly by the fact that cannabis, like tobacco, appears to show its greatest dangers over a long period of time compared with many other drugs.

The growing public perception that marijuana is a safe drug, particularly among teens, can also be explained by the growing, well-financed normalisation campaign that has picked up steam in the past few decades. Promising everything from lower crime to government taxation windfalls, legalisation campaigners have contributed to the increasingly acceptable social norm that cannabis use should be embraced and legitimised. There are of course real concerns stemming around social justice that we should all care about, but many are asking if the wisest route is to repeat for cannabis, the same policy we have had for alcohol. The recent success of legitimisation campaigns about cannabis has had many repercussions.

One of those consequences does not get spoken about often–it is not the societal-level effects of such normalisation, but rather the effects on the individual. How does a casual societal attitude affect the person who does have a cannabis problem and is trying to wrestle with it? And how much do cannabis problems have to do with today's high-potency varieties and the way young people are now ingesting the substance? Beyond the big policy questions that are painted across newspapers and websites today are some more fundamental issues that parents and young people grapple with every day: 'Will I be a hypocrite if I tell my child not to use cannabis even though I once did?' 'Am I a hypocrite for using alcohol in front of my children while I admonish them for using cannabis?' And it is not just parents who deal with hard questions when it comes to this drug. Kids often wonder, 'Is cannabis really that harmful at all?' 'How does cannabis compare with tobacco?' 'Does cannabis make me a safer driver?' 'Unlike heroin, cannabis doesn't kill people, so what is the big deal anyway?'

These questions are often difficult to answer. That is why what Copeland, Rooke, and Matalon have accomplished here is so refreshing–it offers a 'one-stop shop' for parents, kids, elected officials, and anyone interested in putting the rhetoric aside and discovering for themselves what the science says about all of these questions.

Given today's highly polarized debate about drugs and drug policy, it is not surprising that having a civil, rational, science-based discussion about this most discussed, written about, and prevalent illicit drug can be a difficult task. This book, however, is an opportunity for all of us to put our prejudices about cannabis aside and gives us a fresh beginning to start those conversations.

We need more books like this—ones that promote a smart balance between the extremes of either 'tough' or 'lenient' marijuana law policies. That is why former Rhode Island congressman Patrick J. Kennedy and I started a new group called Project SAM—Smart Approaches to Marijuana (<www.learnaboutsam.org>). Project SAM is a collaboration of individuals and organizations seeking marijuana policy that neither incarcerates people with small amounts of marijuana nor creates a profit-driven commercial marijuana industry that aggressively markets the drug. Our desired marijuana policy would reduce marijuana use through prevention, treatment, and smart justice, but it would not cripple marijuana users and low-level dealers with career-ending arrest or incarceration records. This common sense 'middle-ground' approach relies on science, public health, and public safety principles to guide marijuana policy. Legalization opens the door to the development of a massive commercial industry that would target and addict the young and the poor, continuously invent new products to capture segmented markets, steadfastly deny that its products cause any harm to health, safety, or well-being, and make so much money that multibillion -dollar lawsuits would simply be the normal cost of doing business. We can do better. This book gives us the reason why we need to.

Kevin Sabet Ph.D.
Director, Drug Policy Institute and Assistant Professor
University of Florida, College of Medicine
January 2015

Introduction

I slide into the back seat of the cab, weighed down with papers for yet another meeting, pondering how to respond to the inevitable question. As the driver fixes on my reflection in the rear-vision mirror, I hear it coming: 'Where do ya work, love?' Do I have the strength for 'I'm a Professor and the Director of the National Cannabis Prevention and Information Centre' or do I settle for 'I work at a university', hoping he will conclude—as so many do—that a woman of my age will be an administrative officer of some kind and move on. It would be something to be proud of either way, but if I chose the former I could be in for a serious ear-bashing about cannabis being a blessed herb that cures cancer and indeed all life's ills or, just as likely, a horribly dangerous drug that inevitably causes madness and a life of misery.

Cannabis is a drug that inspires religious-like devotion from some users and their advocates, and equally fervent rejection and concern from users who have experienced serious problems, or family and friends who have witnessed the decline of loved ones who have been early, regular and/or heavy users of the drug.

Intense personal experiences aside, it is hardly surprising that the vast majority of people—even health-care professionals—are unaware of, or confused about, what the scientific evidence says about the effects of cannabis: whether it is addictive, more potent, safe, causes schizophrenia, affects driving, and a whole range of other myths abounding on the internet and in the media. In contrast to tobacco and alcohol— or even heroin—all of which have been widely researched from many angles, modern research on cannabis is only about 50 years old. As a result, there is a great deal more to be learnt about this complex drug, our body's natural cannabis receptor systems and their functions, the long-term effects of regular cannabis use, how we can prevent or delay use, and medications that will help to manage cannabis withdrawal and help people to quit successfully.

This book is designed for anyone curious about cannabis: those just interested in knowing more about this controversial drug; those who have used it in the past or do so currently; their friends and family; and anyone who works with cannabis users. It aims to briefly summarise what the best-quality research tells us about the controversial issues that surround this drug. Among the issues dealt with are the impacts of cannabis use on mental health and a chapter devoted to the most common harm associated with long-term regular use of cannabis: addiction. Chapter 6 examines withdrawal: What is the evidence for cannabis dependence? How is it experienced? There is even a quick test for you to check whether or not you meet the criteria for a diagnosis of cannabis use disorder.

In our work over the years, we have had many parents, as well as partners, friends and even children, of heavy cannabis users ask us how they can raise the topic and assist the person to get help without yet another fight and more drama. We have provided, in chapter 8, some techniques to help guide you through these 'difficult' conversations in a way that will help the cannabis user feel less attacked and be more willing to at least consider your concerns. With any luck, they will then be willing to read the chapters that follow about how to make changes in their cannabis use. We talk about how people make and sustain the kinds of behaviour changes required for quitting a long-term habit like regular cannabis use. Chapter 9 provides a guide to consolidating motivation, understanding and managing any withdrawal symptoms, dealing with core symptoms of addiction and developing a plan to sustain change into the future.

This information is based on our combined five decades of experience in developing and researching ways to help cannabis users successfully manage their cannabis use problems. In the mid-1990s, I was a junior supervisor of a colleague's doctoral thesis that examined the nature and existence of cannabis dependence. She had recruited a group of long-term regular cannabis users—not specifically looking for people who thought they might be having problems with their cannabis use, but rather seeking those who smoked at least weekly for three to five years—to follow up for a year (Swift, Hall & Copeland, 2000).

She came to me one day and said some of her participants felt they needed treatment to quit cannabis as they had tried a number of times without long-term success. They felt ashamed that they were struggling, as everyone knew cannabis was not addictive, and they felt like failures. As we tried to think about where to refer them, I did a quick search of the scientific evidence for information on how best to treat people with cannabis problems. At that time, there was only one group in the world publishing research on this topic. As I was then specialising in drug and alcohol treatment for women, I knew there was a lot of treatment research for other drugs, so was shocked at the huge gap around cannabis. I contacted the head of one of the very few cannabis treatment research groups, Professor Roger Roffman at the University of Washington in Seattle, and asked for his advice about doing similar work in Australia. It was a fortuitous contact, as Roger and his colleague Bob Stephens were incredible scientists, hugely compassionate when it came to those with cannabis problems and extremely generous with their time and sharing of materials to help us get started. Roger has now published a book about his experiences (Roffman 2014).

Almost 20 years later, my colleagues and I are still actively involved in developing and testing cannabis interventions and training workers in how to assess and treat cannabis problems. This book is based on that research, and we thank everyone who has helped build that science with us over the years.

To set the book in a wider context, there are many theories of addiction, but they largely fall into three categories: it is a brain disease, a lifestyle choice, or self-medication. This book does not rely on the reader signing up to any underlying theory of addiction that means following a program such as long-term psychotherapy or going to 12-step meetings—although if a reader finds that Alcoholics

Anonymous/Narcotics Anonymous or, where available, Marijuana Anonymous works for them, they should definitely keep attending meetings regularly. Chapters 7 and 9 discuss behaviour change, and the techniques we suggest are based on learning theory, which has the strongest scientific evidence of effectiveness for resolving cannabis problems (Danovitch & Gorelik 2012). While those of us involved in treatment research tend to focus on people who are seeking counselling for their cannabis problems, we shouldn't forget that the majority of people who successfully quit cannabis and stay that way do it by themselves, without any treatment at all. The same is true for alcohol and tobacco problems. That is why we believe that this book will be enough to help many of those who are ready to quit to successfully make that change. For readers who need more personalised assistance, Chapter 9 includes information about telephone and web-based treatments that are free of charge.

A final note about the format of the book: while it is tempting for academics to reference every statement, it doesn't make for easy reading, so we will just include one or two new or key references and a link to the relevant fact sheet or a similar information source on the National Cannabis Prevention and Information Centre's (NCPIC) website for further reading. While we are all currently working at NCPIC, which is supported by the Australian government, the views expressed in this book are entirely our own and do not reflect those of the Australian government or our employer, UNSW Australia.

CHAPTER 1

What you really need to know about cannabis

This chapter comes with a mild warning. It is the closest we get to sounding a bit like a textbook. We have wrestled with how to convey enough information to keep the closet 'potologist' interested (we thought we made up that term, but Google tells us someone beat us to it) without causing everyone else to quietly put the book down and step away.

Let's start with what cannabis is called across various cultures and countries. The most common terms used are dope, pot, grass, mull, blaze, green, ganja or gunja, marijuana, yarndi and weed. If you enjoy knowing more about the scientific and even just plain silly names for cannabis, please look at and add to our Cannabisaurus at <http://cannabis-aur.us>. In the United Kingdom, high-potency cannabis that is usually grown hydroponically is called skunk—especially by the British tabloid newspapers. In the United States, the Mexican Spanish slang term for herbal cannabis, marijuana, is still used even in legislation (see <http://ncpic.org.au/workforce/alcohol-and-other-drug-workers/cannabis-information/factsheets/article/cannabis-or-marijuana>).

Other terms include bud, 420 and puff, among many others. There is quite a subculture that builds around certain terms. For example, 420 arose from the time 4.20 p.m., which was allegedly the time that a group of kids met after school, initially to search for a mythical cannabis crop, but it came to mean the time you start smoking cannabis and now just means cannabis itself. The expression has been worked to death over time, with more cannabis puns—especially about legalisation issues—than we dare try to cover.

Cannabis comes from the cannabis plant, predominantly *Cannabis sativa*, but that strain is sometimes bred with the shorter and bushier strain known as *Cannabis indica*, especially for indoor cultivation. It grows wild in many of the tropical and temperate areas of the world. Cannabis can be grown in almost any climate, and is increasingly cultivated by means of indoor hydroponic technology (growing cannabis indoors using artificial lighting, mineral nutrient solutions and water).

There are some basic facts about the two main chemicals in cannabis that we need to talk about. The chemical family unique to the cannabis plants are called cannabinoids. There are more than 100 of them that we know about, with research identifying new ones all the time. The main active ingredient in cannabis is called delta-9-tetrahydrocannabinol, commonly known as THC. This is the cannabinoid that gives the 'high', and it is also thought to be responsible for the feelings of anxiety and paranoia and other mental health problems that can be experienced when using the drug. The second most common cannabinoid is called cannabidiol or CBD. This is the compound from the cannabis plant that is thought to have the most potential as a medicine. It is important to note that CBD does not produce any high. Its effects are the opposite of THC, and it is known to reduce anxiety and paranoia. The potency of cannabis is determined by the percentage of THC. Usually the more THC the plant has, the less CBD it contains.

Now we have covered the chemistry, we have to add some botany. Cannabis is used in three main forms: the whole plant, resin and oil. The plant preparation of flowering heads (and, less commonly, leaves) is sometimes called marijuana. The purer resin form is known as hashish. The leaves of the plant have the lowest potency, followed by the flowering head. Hashish is made from the resin in the flowering heads, which is separated from the cannabis plant by various techniques. The potency of hashish is highly variable, depending on the technique used to extract the resin. Methods vary from traditional hand-rubbing and rolling to extraction with ice and solvents. Hash oil is released from the cannabis plant by separating the oil with a solvent. The most common solvent is butane, which is why it is called BHO (butane hash oil). This is the most potent cannabis product ever made, and is fortunately not common outside the United States. It varies from a light honey colour to a dark-coloured oil or a waxy substance. In addition to BHO, these extremely high potency preparations are also called dab or shatter. They require a special device with a platform (usually made from a nail head or glass) where the product is placed on a heat source such as a butane torch. The heat releases the THC in a vapour that is then inhaled (along with the gases from the heat source, of course).

All of these forms of cannabis can be smoked, eaten in a variety of products such as butters and cakes, or drunk as teas or in milky drinks. Smoking is the most common method across the world. In Australia, the majority of users mix their cannabis with tobacco in roughly equal proportions (Norberg, MacKenzie & Copeland 2012). This increases the risk of harm to the lungs, and can lead to another problem: nicotine addiction (see <http://ncpic. org.au/workforce/alcohol-and-other-drug-workers/ cannabis-information/factsheets/article/cannabis-and- tobacco-use>). There are interesting national variations regarding whether tobacco is used at all, with smoking cannabis alone being the norm in the United States and New Zealand.

In addition to the special gadgets required to use hash oil, there are many ways in which cannabis can be smoked. A common method is a water pipe or bong (a pipe with a water filtration), especially when cannabis is being shared with others. The metal device that holds the cannabis in the bong or pipe is known as a cone. There is no standard cone but it usually contains about a tenth of a gram (Norberg, MacKenzie and Copeland 2012). A varia- tion is a bucket or gravity bong, which forces the smoke into the lungs as the water is displaced when the smoke- filled bottle is pushed down into the water-filled bucket. When smoking devices have to be improvised with any objects at hand, such as in prisons, crushed soft drink cans and plastic bottles are also used. These methods involve risks, such as exposure to high volumes of smoke, and the burning plastic lining and paint of soft drink cans and bottles.

A more traditional way of smoking cannabis—especially where use is tolerated as part of everyday life—is rolling the cannabis with or without tobacco, in a cigarette called a joint or spliff. An American innovation involves hollowing out the centre of a cheap cigar and packing it with cannabis—known as a blunt. The very rapid expansion of medicinal cannabis in the United States has seen an increase in its use in various foods and the use of vaporisers, which are devices that are used to extract and inhale cannabis vapour without having to burn the cannabis. See <http://ncpic.org.au/workforce/alcohol-and-other-drug-workers/cannabis-information/factsheets/article/vaporisers> for further information on this method of use, as it does not eliminate the risks of inhaling cannabis products as many believe.

The many ways of using cannabis are only limited by its fatty consistency, which means that it is not injected as it can't be dissolved into a solution. For those who have read scientific papers about THC being injected in human and animal studies, it is synthetic THC that is being used, not the stuff you smoke.

What happens when you smoke cannabis?

Most people who use cannabis do so to experience a sense of euphoria and relaxation, known as the 'high'. Cannabis causes changes in the user's mood, and also affects how they think and perceive the environment—for example, the experience of listening to music can be altered and more intense, and time perception can be altered.

Cannabis does not fit into the general drug categories such as stimulant, depressant or hallucinogen, as it has all of these effects depending on the dose of THC. Smoked cannabis gets THC acting on the brain within seconds, with the effect peaking within 20 minutes and lasting three to four hours. When cannabis is eaten, the effects are delayed, reaching a peak three to four hours after use and lasting around six to eight hours (EMCDDA 2008). This is why people—especially those inexperienced with taking cannabis in this way—can take more than they intended and experience really unpleasant and scary symptoms, such as anxiety, paranoia and hallucinations. There are plenty of stories on the web of even the most experienced cannabis smokers coming to grief after eating baked products containing cannabis.

What are the effects of cannabis?

We are all familiar with users' stories about why they use—mostly boredom and liking the effect—but what does the science tell us? The psychological effects of cannabis include the euphoric high feeling, but also anxiety, depersonalisation (not feeling yourself or feeling unreal) and an aggravation of psychotic states. It can heighten sensory perception, distort the sense of time and space, and cause hallucinations. With the high-potency hash oils being used now, hallucinations are becoming more common. It also has sedative effects, which can make the effects of other drugs that also have sedative effects—such as alcohol and many medications—more severe. In terms of mental performance, it can cause clouding of judgement, memory loss and generally impaired performance. It also affects motor functions, such as balance and coordination. The other effects include stimulation of the appetite (known as 'the munchies'), analgesia (pain relief) and, of course, addiction with long-term use. There are also a range of effects on the rest of the body, including dry mouth, red eyes, increased heart rate if an inexperienced user, variable effects on blood pressure, decreased sperm count and motility in males, and suppression of ovulation and other hormonal effects in females. This summary of effects was adapted from an article by Kumar, Chambers and Pertwee (2001).

How does the body deal with cannabis?

This section is quite technical. The psychoactive component of cannabis, THC, was only identified in the 1960s, and it wasn't until the 1990s that the existence of our body's natural endogenous cannabinoid system (ECS) was discovered. The term 'endogenous' is used because it is produced within our bodies and not taken in from outside. This is not unique to cannabis, as our bodies also have natural receptors to deal with opioids such as codeine and heroin. This endogenous opioid system produces compounds known as endorphins that, when released during the stress of exercise for example, produce the so-called runner's high. In the same way, we have an endogenous cannabinoid system that produces compounds which have similar effects to very tiny doses of THC.

The best known of these natural cannabinoids is Anandamide. One way to understand this in a very stripped down way is to think of the ECS as a series of locks waiting to be opened by the chemical key contained by any cannabinoid. It is usually opened by an endogenous cannabinoid such as Anandamide to allow other chemical reactions to take place within the brain and body. If you add THC from outside the body, however, it will be preferred by the lock, as it opens it more easily. As a result, if you keep taking THC into the body, it stops making endogenous cannabinoids as all the locks have already been opened by THC.

As the body adapts to the locks being more fully opened by THC, the system adapts and more THC is needed to achieve the high feeling. This need to take more THC to get an effect is called tolerance, and it is one of the first signs of addiction. This also explains why regular, heavy users experience withdrawal. When THC is first stopped, the locks that are used to being fully open suddenly have no key to open them at all, and the chemical reactions that rely on that process don't happen anymore. This is experienced as withdrawal, and will be discussed in more detail in later chapters. Physical withdrawal lasts as long as it takes for those endogenous cannabinoids, which had been turned off because they had no work to do when there was lots of THC around, to get back into production. This rebalancing will then open those locks at a lower cannabinoid level, and allow the natural system to function.

The location of the two best-known cannabinoid receptor systems within the body explains why cannabis has the effects it does. The first is known as CB1, and these receptors are mostly found in the brain and nervous system, while CB2 receptors are abundant in the immune and reproductive systems. The science is very new, and developing rapidly to shed light on the effects of taking in high levels of THC and other cannabinoids on the short- and long-term functioning of these two systems. The parts of the brain where CB1 receptors are found explain why its use is a positive or rewarding experience after the first couple of times, before use becomes regular. The brain systems that mediate the effects of alcohol and opioids are in the same parts of the brain as the cannabis receptors, so it is not surprising that problems with addiction to cannabis arise after regular (weekly or more often) use. One of these chemical systems is the dopaminergic system, which is also involved in disease processes such as schizophrenia. While this seems complicated enough, it is actually very much a simplified overview of this complex system and its interactions. Those interested in further reading should consult Atakan (2012).

What about cannabis and drug testing?

If cannabis is a controversial drug, then random drug testing for cannabis use is a barbecue-stopper. The following is a brief guide to what the science says about how the body deals with cannabis and how its use can be detected. The most important thing to know is that it is highly variable, and also depends on how much is used and over what period of time. This comes with the usual disclaimer that this general information cannot be relied upon for any individual to ensure that they will not have their cannabis use detected in workplace or other drug-testing regimes.

One of the ways in which cannabis is different from other drugs is that it is highly fat soluble. The levels of THC in the blood usually fall rapidly about half an hour after a single use. The body breaks it down into more than a hundred different metabolites, which are stored in fatty tissue and excreted slowly. The rate of excretion depends on the amount of fat in the body, as well as factors that break down fat cells, such as starvation and heavy exercise. Repeated use of cannabis causes these metabolites to build up, and they can take many weeks to clear the body. It is these metabolites that are routinely tested for in 'dip stick' and laboratory tests for cannabis use, as THC itself is only rarely detected in the urine.

In Australia and some European countries, there is random roadside drug testing for THC using saliva testing. In oral fluid (mostly saliva) tests, it is THC that is the target compound. In controlled studies of cannabis smoking, it was found that THC initially is rapidly eliminated from oral fluid in the first hour or two after use, but this rate gradually declines, leaving scientifically detectable levels in some people over days. In general, however, it is below the cut-off levels used in drug testing after six hours (Lee & Huestis 2013). Given the high degree of variability of THC elimination in saliva, it is best to wait 24 hours after cannabis use to be sure your driving skills are not impaired and you won't test positive on a saliva test. It is also very important that your mouth not be contaminated with any cannabis product—even if you didn't inhale!

A final way in which cannabis use can be detected is via hair testing as, like all drugs, it leaves a residue as the hair grows. This is only used in forensic and research settings, as it is expensive and easily avoided by shaving the hair where there are penalties for testing positive. Breath analysis to detect cannabis use is now being developed and if proven valid and realiable will be a logical addition to roadside alcohol breath testing.

It's legal, right?

Cannabis legalisation, and the potential of cannabinoids as medicines, are two of the most common and complex cannabis issues that are mentioned in the media. It is outside the scope of this book to have a meaningful discussion about these important topics. The relevant legal status of cannabis obviously depends on the location of the reader. With the exception of Uruguay and the two US states of Washington and Colorado, across the world it is illegal to use, possess or sell cannabis, but the penalties for cannabis offences differ. While cannabis possession has been decriminalised in many countries, it is important to remember that decriminalisation should not be confused with legalisation. Decriminalisation means that criminal sanctions for cannabis possession for personal use only (limit usually stated) have largely been removed. Although the Netherlands is reputed to have legalised cannabis because openly selling cannabis in 'coffee shops' is largely tolerated, it too has merely decriminalised use of the drug. Ironically, the cannabis products that are illegal coming in the coffee shop's back door are legal going out the front door when sold to the customer!

Now we've got Cannabis 101 covered, let's move on to those frequently asked questions so you'll be armed with what the science says when working on your motivation to quit or trying to convince someone else that they need to think more seriously about their cannabis use.

CHAPTER 2

Cannabis myths: The drug

Despite being used by humans for thousands of years—usually under tight control by religious leaders and healers of various types—there is a special level of mystery and political fervour surrounding cannabis. This may be partly explained by its complexity—given that it contains more than 500 chemicals and around 100 unique cannabinoids (Pertwee 2006). Very strong beliefs about the need for the legalisation of cannabis can be held for a variety of reasons. These include a strong commitment to civil liberties in general, social justice concerns about the harsh policing of cannabis laws in some countries or a desire to have cannabis use free of legal consequences for the individual or their loved ones.

While we may share some of these concerns, to varying extents, it is very worrying that the lobby groups and individuals supporting legalisation of cannabis (and all drugs) get plenty of media space to vigorously promote ill-informed pro-cannabis messages and blindly deny any evidence of cannabis-related harms. We have been in the uncomfortable position of falsely being seen as promoting harsh cannabis laws and being motivated to promote propaganda rather than evidence. It is also tough to be wrongly seen as denying the terminally ill cannabinoids as medicine, given our public calls for research on pharmaceutical cannabis products for this purpose. Aside from the mentally ill and severely intoxicated, the most violent hate mail comes from the cannabis entrepreneurs who stand to make a great deal of money from legalised cannabis, and don't want any attention to cannabis-related harms as they attempt to drive public perceptions in their preferred direction. The number and calibre of poisonous emails, internet posts and death threats have been astounding– and don't speak well of their author's ability to construct a rational argument, spell or use grammar correctly!

As you can imagine, over the years we have been asked thousands of questions by people in very different situations about cannabis. These questions are frequently prefaced by an oft-cited myth. This chapter summarises some of the most common myths and uncertainties surrounding cannabis use, apart from those that concern directly mental health, which are addressed in the following chapter. We hope that separating the myths from the evidence as it currently stands will be useful in a range of ways, and that it will help you to get the most out of this book.

Myth no. 1: Everyone uses cannabis

If you took on board the messages in some of the mass media, you would believe that every young person is stoned. On the other hand, if most of your friends use cannabis, you might also come to believe that it is normal. So what does the evidence tell us?

Cannabis is the most widely produced and used illicit drug in the world, with approximately 180.6 million people, or 3.9 per cent of the world's population aged 15–64 years reporting use in the most recent surveys (UNODC 2013). Its consumption patterns are unevenly distributed, with the highest prevalence rates in New Zealand, the Pacific Islands, Australia and North America. Global patterns of use differ: while use appeared to be stable or in decline in Canada, Western Europe and New Zealand after peaks were observed in the late 1990s, trends towards increased use have recently been reported in Africa, Eastern Europe, South and Central America, Asia and, in very recent surveys, Australia and the United States.

Cannabis use is most common among young adults, predominating among Australians aged 18–29 years (21 per cent reported past-year use), North Americans aged 18–25 years (19 per cent reported past-month use) and 15–24-year-olds in the European Union (an average of 15 per cent reported last-year use). There are some trends emerging about patterns of use. These include that people are starting use first at a younger age, now on average 18.5 years in Australia (AIHW 2011) for those in the population aged over 14 years. Similar data are not readily available for international comparisons; however, historically the age of first cannabis use has been dropping in most Western countries. In the United States, the average age at first cannabis use was 19 years in the early 1970s; this decreased to 17 years in the 1990s and by 1999 was 16.4 years for males and 17.6 years for females (Gfroerer, Wu & Penne 2002).

Australian and US national data also indicate increases in recent cannabis use among 50-59-year-olds, perhaps partially reflecting the ageing of that group who used cannabis when it first became more widely popular in the 1970s. The most concerning pattern is frequent use–that is, weekly or more often. Recent US data reported that 5.4 million persons aged 12 or older had used cannabis on a daily or almost daily basis in the past 12 months, which was a significant increase from 2006 (SAMHSA 2013). In Australia, there are about 300,000 daily cannabis users (AIHW 2011).

In summary, we have to be concerned because cannabis use is increasing, as are patterns of regular heavy use. It is worrying, for example, that in Australia–given the success of anti-tobacco and related public health campaigns–adolescents aged 14-19 years are now more likely to have smoked cannabis than tobacco (AIHW 2011). A more optimistic way of looking at it is that the vast majority of Australians do not now use (90 per cent) and never have used (65 per cent) cannabis. This pattern is even more marked in the US where a recent survey of high school students found that in the past 30 days 23.4 per cent reported using marijuana compared with 15.7 per cent reporting having smoked cigarettes (MMWR, 2014).

Myth no. 2: Cannabis today is a different drug

When considering the issue of how strong cannabis is now compared with a few decades ago, it is easy to conjure the image of an argument between a parent and teenager that goes something like this:

Parent: 'You're smoking pot?? Don't you realise how stupid that is?'

Teenager: 'But you smoked pot when you were my age. I guess that must mean YOU were stupid.'

Parent: 'That's completely different. It's a totally different drug now—kids don't realise that the stuff that's around today is 30 times stronger than what we smoked back in the 70s.'

This is a very widely held view about the cannabis of today. But is there any truth to it? Well, sort of. A number of changes to cannabis and its consumption patterns that have occurred over the last several years have led to the drug being more potent now than it was in the past. First, while cannabis users in the 1970s were most likely to smoke the leaves of the plant, cannabis users today pretty much exclusively smoke the more potent flowering tops, or buds, of the plant.

The way in which cannabis is grown also affects the amount of THC in the plant, and therefore the potency. It is becoming more common for female plants to be grown in isolation, so the flowering tops of the plant remain unfertilised. These unfertilised flowering tops, known as sinsemilla, have particularly high THC levels. Cross-breeding and genetic modification can also produce strains of the cannabis plant that lead to higher levels of THC. As discussed in the previous chapter, hash oil and resin have much higher levels of THC than plant material.

So could these changes that have occurred to cannabis in recent years really have resulted in a 30-fold increase in its potency that a politician once claimed? Well no, but it has definitely increased over the years. A recent analysis of cannabis that had been confiscated by police from users found with 15 grams (about half an ounce) or less under the New South Wales Cannabis Cautioning Scheme, found that the average THC content was 15 per cent and had almost no CBD (Swift et al. 2013). This echoes trends reported in other countries regarding the use of high-potency cannabis with very low CBD content. The University of Mississippi has been monitoring cannabis potency in the United States since 1960 from similar types of law-enforcement seizures. It reports that the average THC potency had doubled in recent years.

A further myth that is commonly believed is that cannabis grown in the outdoors, known as bush, is a safer and less potent drug than cannabis grown indoors—which is often referred to as hydro. This is short for hydroponic, which suggests water is the only medium, but soils and other materials are often used as well as a range of chemicals to boost growth and reduce disease. Cannabis produced by criminal gangs in commercial grow houses may also contain more contaminants such as mould or pesticides. The recent study by Swift and colleagues (2013), however, found no difference between outdoor and indoor cannabis in terms of its potency or level of CBD. It should be remembered, though, that simply focusing on cannabis potency rather than patterns of use may obscure the fact that young, regular users are most at risk of cannabis-related harm.

Myth no. 3: Bongs are safer than joints—aren't they?

In many countries, cannabis is most commonly smoked in either a joint or a bong (water pipe). Although the use of water in a smoking apparatus has a long tradition, the origin of the water pipe is unclear. There is increasing evidence to suggest that bongs were first used to smoke cannabis in eastern and southern Africa before the introduction of tobacco. However, others believe that water pipes originated in China or Persia, and were first used there to smoke tobacco.

The word 'bong' is an adaptation of the Thai word *baung*, which refers to a cylindrical pipe or tube cut from bamboo. One of the earliest recorded uses of the word in the West is in the *McFarland Thai-English Dictionary*, published in 1944, which describes one of the meanings of 'bong' in the Thai language as 'a bamboo water pipe for smoking *kancha*, tree, hashish, or the hemp-plant'.

When a water pipe is used, cannabis smoke is cooled by travelling over the water, which reduces its temperature and harshness on the throat and lungs, thus minimising the burning feeling to the smoker's throat.

One of the major harms linked to cannabis use is the potential respiratory damage caused by smoking. Considering the popularity of smoking cannabis via a water pipe, it is surprising how little research has been conducted on this route of administration and the potential respiratory harms associated with the practice.

Many believe that smoking cannabis is relatively free from harm, particularly when compared with tobacco. Regardless of how cannabis is smoked, however, four distinct harms to respiratory health have been identified as a result of cannabis smoking:

◆ Cannabis and tobacco smoke include a similar range of pro-inflammatory and carcinogenic substances.

- The damaging effects of inhaling cannabis smoke are similar to those from tobacco smoke.
- Acute exposure to cannabis smoke results in small reductions in lung function, accompanied by respiratory symptoms such as a cough and wheeze.
- With longer term exposure, tobacco and cannabis smoking have additive effects on lung function and respiratory symptoms.

When it comes to the use of the water pipe specifically, some users believe that the bong reduces exposure to potentially toxic materials, such as tar, due to the smoke being 'filtered' by the water. This has been disproved, with a number of studies finding that bongs do not in fact provide this protection. The most important of these was a study partly sponsored by the National Organization for the Reform of Marijuana Laws (NORML), which tested smoke from seven different sources—a variety of joints, bongs and vaporisers. Three water pipes were used in the study: a standard bong, a small portable device with a folding pipestream and a battery-operated model with a motorised paddle that mixed the smoke with the water. The study looked at two components of the smoke—tars (waste by-products of burning) and cannabinoids (compounds distinctive to cannabis including THC, as well as CBN and CBD)—and aimed to determine the efficacy of various smoking devices at reducing the concentration of tars relative to cannabinoids (Gieringer 2000).

The results showed that, contrary to popular belief, using a bong did not appear to protect smokers from the harmful tars in cannabis smoke. In fact, the water pipes filtered out more psychoactive THC than they did tars, which meant that users had to smoke more to reach their desired effect.

Of the three devices tested, the pipe that mixed the smoke with water scored by far the worst. This led the authors to conclude that water filtration is actually counterproductive because water appears to absorb THC more readily than tars.

Myth no. 4: Cannabis is a 'gateway' drug and inevitably leads to other illegal drug use

An interesting argument against the use of cannabis is one that doesn't relate directly to the effects of taking the drug: some people claim that cannabis 'opens the gateway' to harder drug use. There are arguments for and against the view that cannabis is a gateway drug. Let's explore both sides, then consider whether it really matters one way or the other.

Those who claim that cannabis is in fact a gateway drug point out that people who have used cannabis are way more likely to try other so-called harder drugs such as heroin and cocaine in the future. For example, one study of twins who were tracked from adolescence into adulthood found that those who used cannabis in their teens were much more likely to use a variety of other drugs down the track. This finding was apparent even after accounting for genetic and environmental factors that could influence drug use (Agrawal et al. 2004).

It is also relevant that animal studies have found regular cannabis use can have pharmacological effects on brain function that encourage the use of other drugs, and this may account for the apparent gateway effect of cannabis use. For example, in one study of adolescent rats, half of the rats were pre-treated with cannabinoids before being trained to self-administer heroin. Those pre-treated with cannabinoids self-administered significantly higher doses of heroin relative to those not pre-treated with cannabinoids (Ellgren, Spano & Hurd 2007).

Some people who have used cannabis and then moved on to other drugs have offered explanations for this that are consistent with the gateway theory. For example, some people say that they tried harder drugs after tolerance to cannabis built up and the effect of the drug began to lessen. The user may then try stronger drugs because cannabis no longer 'does the job'. Other people have said that the exaggerated media portrayals of cannabis harms have contributed to it being a gateway drug. According to this argument, if a young person is told any cannabis use makes you crazy, but does not see this happening to their friends then—in contradiction to media drug messages about cannabis—uses it a few times with no problem, they are likely to conclude that any anti-drug message is also wrong and then turn to harder drugs. Other people simply say that smoking cannabis lowered their inhibitions to try harder drugs.

An additional concern is that the markets for cannabis are often mixed with other illicit drugs. Dealers prefer to sell powdered drugs as they are easier to conceal and have more profit, so they encourage cannabis users to try them. While this makes sense in some ways, the vast majority of users report that they obtain their cannabis from friends and family, not from commercial dealers.

The flipside of the argument also offers some persuasive evidence countering the gateway theory. Some studies that have carefully ruled out the effects of other factors that could influence both cannabis use and subsequent use of harder drugs have concluded that whether adolescents who use cannabis will go on to use harder drugs depends more on other factors, such as mental health, employment, education and ethnicity, rather than on the cannabis use itself (Van Gundy & Rebellon 2010).

People who use cannabis and don't believe it is a gateway drug have pointed out that the vast majority of people who use cannabis at a younger age don't continue to use cannabis in the future, let alone move on to hard drugs. Another common refutation of the gateway theory is that other drugs, such as tobacco and alcohol, regularly precede cannabis use. One cannabis user commented that, 'For me personally I look at cigarettes as my gateway—I smoked them before anything and it was easy to put a joint to my lips because I already knew how to inhale.' Thus the same reasoning that leads to the view that cannabis is a gateway drug should also lead to the view that alcohol and tobacco are gateway drugs. Interestingly, recent animal evidence suggests that THC may increase the addictive effects of nicotine in rats—acting as a reverse gateway (Panlilio et al. 2013).

A large multinational study explored this question, and found that cannabis is the most available drug after tobacco and alcohol in most countries. They reported that where other drugs are more available than cannabis, they are more likely to be next in the sequence among those that progress to 'harder' drug use (Degenhardt et al. 2010).

Overall, it should be remembered that the vast majority of cannabis users do not go on to use other illegal drugs. It is most likely that the same personal and socio-economic characteristics that make it more likely for an individual to be willing to use an illegal drug are the same for cannabis as for other drugs—that is, a common factor is the cause. There is evidence, however, that cannabis could act as an important stepping stone to other illicit drug use for some people.

Myth no. 5: Mixing your drugs—cannabis with alcohol and tobacco

> Beer then grass, you're on your ass;
> grass then beer you're in the clear!

This sounds like a very simple rule of thumb for mixing cannabis with alcohol; but let's look at this piece of 'advice' a little more closely. Is it really safe to mix alcohol with cannabis as long as you use cannabis before drinking alcohol? Anecdotally, drinking alcohol before using cannabis gives people a worse reaction than using the substances in the reverse order. People have described the experience of drinking and smoking cannabis in ways such as, 'If I get wasted and then decide to smoke, I get the spins real bad and end up puking (vomiting),' and 'Have definitely gotten obliterated from using marijuana then alcohol. I've also seen it cause someone to vomit in an *Exorcist*-type fashion.'

It is important to bear in mind, however, that the negative effects of mixing cannabis with alcohol can occur regardless of which substance is used first. When people smoke cannabis and drink alcohol at the same time, they can experience nausea and vomiting, or they can react with panic, anxiety or paranoia. Mixing cannabis with alcohol can increase the risk of vulnerable people experiencing psychotic symptoms. There is some evidence to support the theory that having alcohol in your blood causes a faster absorption of THC. This can lead to the cannabis having a much stronger effect than it would normally have, and can result in 'greening out' (feeling sick from cannabis) or 'chucking a whitey', a term commonly referred to in a situation where people go very pale and feel very sick and vomit after smoking cannabis (see section in Chapter 3 on greening out).

Another drug that is very commonly used in combination with cannabis is tobacco—people may smoke cannabis and tobacco separately, mix their cannabis with tobacco and smoke the two substances simultaneously, or do both. Tobacco and cannabis smoke both contain harmful chemicals, including carcinogens that are absorbed when inhaled. This exposes the smoker's lungs to greater risks of developing major respiratory diseases and cancer. Several studies have found that smoking both cannabis and tobacco tends to lead to greater problems than smoking cannabis alone. These problems range from worse physical health, to a higher rate of psychological problems, to a tendency to use more cannabis overall (Rooke et al. 2013). The British Lung Foundation has estimated that smoking three joints of cannabis a day is equivalent to a pack of 20 cigarettes in airways damage without including any tobacco smoked in the joints (see <www.blf.org.uk/Files/5cbdf46e-8c70-4e75.../A_Smoking_Gun.pdf>).

Another issue that can arise for people who use tobacco to mix with cannabis is unwittingly becoming addicted to nicotine as well. Adult smokers who use cannabis make fewer tobacco smoking cessation attempts, and are less likely to have quit smoking. In addition, those who smoked cannabis and tobacco chose to quit tobacco significantly later than non-cannabis users (Ford, Vu & Anthony 2002), thus exposing themselves to greater harms. It is often the case that cannabis smokers can hold very negative views about cigarette smoking while not recognising that if they smoke cannabis mixed with tobacco regularly, they are effectively smokers (Banbury et al. 2013). Ironically, it is in countries like Australia, where cannabis is usually mixed with tobacco, that people cry, 'There's no cannabis withdrawal—it's just nicotine withdrawal!' This very persistent myth is addressed in Chapter 6, dealing with cannabis withdrawal.

Overall, if you choose to mix tobacco with cannabis, it is important to be aware of all the hidden traps that can lead to health problems as well as addiction to both cannabis and tobacco.

Myth no. 6: Cannabis unleashes my creativity

Some people say that using cannabis can help them think differently and be more creative. Unfortunately, though, long-term use of cannabis can have an effect opposite to opening the mind, by limiting a person's desire to do new activities, think about new things or meet new people. Many people who have used cannabis long term say that they feel their thinking has become noticeably stunted by the drug. On the other hand, people who stop using cannabis after long-term use often say that their way of thinking has expanded since they stopped using.

So is long-term loss of creativity a worthwhile tradeoff for the immediate feeling of enhanced creativity a person has just after smoking cannabis? It is unlikely, as the question of whether cannabis can even make people more creative in the short term is a prickly one. Although using cannabis can lead to a feeling of enhanced creativity, creative output may not reflect this feeling very closely. This example of a poem written by a person when they were stoned gives an illustration of this point.

Killing Time—By Anonymous Stoner

Waiting, not hating,
Sitting, chilling,
Time killing,
Toking and choking.
Old man pops,
He called the cops.
We said 'yeah right'
And took off with fright.
We got away,
Kept them at bay.
It was late in May.
Us, toking in an alleyway.
I gave the bowl a tap.
It was cached.
We took a nap,
We were smashed.

Source: Marijuana.com forum

Okay, it's true that it might have been possible to find a higher quality poem written by someone under the influence of cannabis. Nevertheless, an interesting point remains: when giving feedback on this poem, people who were stoned thought that the poem was much better than those who were sober. Jack S. Margolis, author of *A Child's Garden of Grass* and a regular cannabis smoker, described it well when he wrote:

> There is no such thing as a profound revelation when stoned! At the time of the thought, you may think that when you reveal it the universe will shake, but if you recall it later when you're straight, you'll laugh at its insignificance.

Myth no. 7: Cannabis and motivation

Some people worry that prolonged and heavy cannabis use can cause a person to become withdrawn, sluggish, disinterested and unmotivated—a collection of symptoms that has often been called the amotivational syndrome. Amotivational syndrome has been described as a set of characteristics that include general apathy, loss of productivity, difficulty in carrying out long-term plans, lethargy, depression and an inability to concentrate and sustain attention. While people describe it as a syndrome, it is actually difficult to define. In fact, many who have looked at the state of the scientific evidence have concluded that the symptoms of amotivational syndrome are mostly due to chronic intoxication with varying degrees of depression (Copeland, Gerber & Swift 2006). In addition, anthropological studies of long-term daily cannabis smokers in Jamaica and Costa Rica failed to find evidence of the syndrome. There are lots of problems with studying amotivational syndrome, as it relies on the user's memory of their mood and work history, and it is difficult to disentangle from being stoned a lot. Where we do see more common reports of an amotivational problem is among those who are seeking treatment for their cannabis problems, where failure to achieve life goals is often mentioned as a reason for quitting. This is an anonymous quote from a blog on this condition:

> I have been smoking pot for almost ten years now. I have been a heavy smoker for the better part of that time. I will say that I believe based on my experiences that there definitely is a motivational deficit with heavy use . . . I also think a lot depends on other factors like environment, genetics and overall health. However I think despite those somewhat predetermined factors, when anyone crosses that threshold into heavy use (a point which is different for everyone) the amotivational effects become steadily more present . . . my symptoms have been basically textbook amotivational syndrome—apathy, lack of energy and irritability. For all the know-it-all pot advocates out there who don't believe it causes motivational problems try smoking 3 to 5 joints throughout the day for a few days and see if you notice it.

It appears that while many people who are in treatment complain of the effects of cannabis use on motivation, there is no compelling evidence to support the existence of a generalised amotivational syndrome associated with cannabis use. But if you are using cannabis regularly and find that you are experiencing symptoms of lower motivation, it might be useful to try going without using for a while to see whether you notice any difference. See <http://ncpic.org.au/ncpic/publications/factsheets/article/cannabis-and-motivation>.

CHAPTER 3

Cannabis myths: Health and safety

Many of the most strongly held beliefs about cannabis—whether positive or negative—are about its effects on health and safety, including activities such as driving. This chapter addresses some of the myths about the health-related harms associated with cannabis use and the next chapter focuses on the evidence about its effects on mental health.

Myth no. 1: Cannabis is good for asthma

Just like all good myths, this is based on a half fact! Cannabis used to be advertised as a treatment for asthma before the development of modern medicine. This may have been because of a reduction in constriction of the airways (bronchospasm) and an initial opening of the airway immediately following use. These outcomes of cannabis smoking for this effect are thought to be modest and much less effective than using medicine such as salbutamol or terbutaline (Ventolin, Asmol, Bricanyl) (Tashkin 2013).

This initial relief from bronchospasm is only short lived, and is not experienced after a few weeks of regular smoking. This in itself wouldn't be such a bad thing if it were the only drawback. But on top of this, smoking cannabis can severely impact the respiratory system over the long term. Studies have found that cannabis smokers experience increased respiratory concerns, such as bronchitis, chronic cough or wheeze, and increased mucus or sputum. Cannabis smokers also have an increased risk of developing emphysema, and have been found to have lung cell mutations that precede cancer (Aldington et al. 2007; Tashkin 1999).

People who have used cannabis over the long term often report an increase in respiratory problems consistent with what the research has shown. Take, for example, the experience of an asthmatic who found the effects of cannabis on his asthma evolved in a negative way after repeated use:

> I'm an asthmatic, and smoke cannabis often. Earlier on, every time I smoked my breathing became easier while I was smoking and also right after. But then for the next few days I would notice it was a little worse than normal. Lately my asthma has become more severe—to the point that my inhaler won't work. Instead I'm breathing through a nebuliser about ten times a day. Other than smoking weed, my living has become extremely reduced due to the asthma. If I'd known weed was going to do this to me over time, I swear I never would've touched the stuff. Now it seems too late as no matter what I do, I just can't seem to stop using. It's the only thing I enjoy and the only thing that seems to help for a little while.

Although cannabis can offer short-term relief of breathing difficulties associated with asthma, over the long term the smoke from cannabis will only cause damage to the respiratory system, making asthma worse and perhaps leading to other serious health concerns.

Myth no. 2: Cannabis helps me sleep

It is very common for people to use cannabis at night in the belief that it will help them sleep well. In fact, cannabis is frequently touted as a natural sleep aid by seemingly professional sources. This online US advertisement for medical cannabis is a classic example of this:

> **Can't Sleep? Medical Marijuana Can Help Treat Your Insomnia**
>
> Many people fail to realize how lack of sleep can have a negative effect on their life. Insomnia is not only the cause of poor health; it can also greatly reduce your productivity at work and when left untreated, it can even lead to death.
>
> Although there are several over the counter drugs available to help people fall asleep, many of these products cause drowsiness during the day—not to mention other potential medical complications. There are many insomnia sufferers who complain of feeling tired and sluggish during the day after using sleeping aids.
>
> The good news is you no longer have to settle for harmful sleeping aids. There is a safe and effective alternative known as medical marijuana. Medical marijuana has worked wonders for many victims of insomnia.

It is important to note that medical marijuana is a natural alternative that doesn't have the dangerous effects that many sleeping aids have. More importantly, medical marijuana doesn't make you feel sluggish and fatigued. As a matter of fact, after consuming medical marijuana, it helps you to fall into a relaxing slumber. When you awake, you'll feel well rested and revived.

Ad by Medical Marijuana ID.com <http://medical-marijuana-id.com/medical-marijuana-blog/marijuana-id-cards/cant-sleep-medical-marijuana-can-help-treat-your-insomnia>.

Unfortunately, advertisements such as these ignore the downside of using cannabis to aid sleep. First, aside from all the known negative outcomes linked with using cannabis, the evidence that cannabis can significantly help sleep, even in the short term, is not that convincing. A number of studies have investigated the effects of using cannabis before sleeping, and outcomes have been mixed. While some studies have found that taking cannabis before sleeping increases sleep time and quality, other studies have found the opposite effect (Gates, Albertella & Copeland 2014). At the moment, there is no convincing evidence that cannabis is good for sleep problems. There may also be an effect on newborn babies as studies show cannabis use during pregnancy affects babies sleep, with more irregular sleep and faster arousal time.

More importantly, the long-term effect of using cannabis for sleep is cannabis dependence and the inability to enjoy a restful sleep without cannabis. One recent study found that sleep problems are the primary symptom of cannabis withdrawal (Allsop et al. 2012). People who have been using cannabis regularly for a period of time often say that when they try to stop using, their sleeping problems are the main factor that undermines their efforts, and they often start up again just for a restful night's sleep. This extract is from one of our research participants who was attempting to quit cannabis. It provides a good summary of the damage cannabis can inflict on sleep when used long term:

> I quit smoking weed a few months ago, and am still having a lot of trouble sleeping. Even if I manage to eventually get to sleep I'll wake up at just about nothing. I was up at 2.15 this morning and couldn't get back to sleep. I lay in bed until 5.30 am when I got up and forced myself out for a walk. I have been exercising each day to get myself tired. No change. And my dreams (more like nightmares) are scary and so weird! I wake up with sweats and feel like I'm freaking out. How can this be after three months? All I smoked was a few cones each night so it's not like my use was that out of control. I never had trouble sleeping in my life, til I tried to quit weed. Every time I try and stop I end up starting it up again, all so I can go to sleep.

While cannabis, like alcohol, can seem an appealing option for relaxation and sleep in the short term, the effects of repeatedly using cannabis tend to be the opposite. Anyone considering using cannabis to help them sleep should seriously consider the long-term tradeoff they are making.

Myth no. 3: Cannabis fries your brain

While most people agree that cannabis can make you feel mentally slower at the time of use, and perhaps for a short time afterwards, whether or not regular use of cannabis can cause long-term damage to the brain is a much more controversial issue. While many long-term cannabis users are adamant that their use has had no ill-effect on their thinking, others believe that they have experienced very noticeable impairment that has failed to subside even after months of abstaining from cannabis. Take, for example, an email sent to us from a cannabis user who was concerned that her long-term use had permanently 'fried' her brain:

> Four months ago I quit pot cold turkey after using almost every day since I was 16 (I'm now 27). After going through withdrawal for the first month, I began to notice positive changes in my life from how I felt physically to my emotional wellbeing. There's just one major problem though—after four months without using pot, my brain still has parts of it that feel like they've died. It's as if those places in my brain want to work and are trying to work but there's some kind of blockage. It's difficult to explain. What I am wondering is, will my brain start to feel normal if I go longer without pot or have I permanently fried it?

Many people who quit cannabis after years of regular use experience feelings of cognitive impairment for a period of time after quitting. But what about over the long term? Although the experience would generally be much more subtle than the brain having parts that 'feel dead', recent studies have shown that regular long-term use of cannabis does appear to damage the brain and impair cognitive function. For example, one study used magnetic resonance imaging (MRI) to test for brain abnormalities in fifteen long-term heavy cannabis users with no history of other drug abuse or neurologic/mental disorder. The regions of the brain studied were two that are rich in cannabis receptors: the hippocampus and the amygdala. The researchers compared the MRI results with those of fifteen individuals who were similar to the test group except that they didn't use cannabis, finding that the cannabis users had reduced hippocampal and amygdala volumes. In addition to this, the amount of exposure to cannabis was negatively associated with hippocampal volume—that is, the greater the cannabis exposure, the lower the hippocampal volume (Yücel et al. 2008).

In another study, 1037 people were followed from birth to age 38, and took intelligence tests at ages 13 (prior to onset of cannabis use) and 38. Those in the study who had used cannabis persistently from adolescence showed a decline in intelligence scores. Further, quitting cannabis after using persistently in adolescence did not completely restore intellectual functioning with a drop in IQ on average of six points and a deficit noticeable to those close to the individual (Meier et al. 2012).

Overall, while the effects of using smaller amounts of cannabis are not currently known, research on cannabis use and brain functioning suggests that heavy, long-term use can damage the brain and lead to impaired cognitive functioning. This seems to be especially true if persistent use begins during adolescence when the brain is not yet fully developed.

Myth no. 4: Too much cannabis = greening out?

'Greening out' refers to the situation where people feel sick after smoking cannabis. People can go pale and sweaty, feel dizzy and nauseous, and may even start vomiting. Some people experience a racing heart, hallucinations and feelings of panic. Many experiences of greening out are similar to the one described below by 'Mike', who had used cannabis on many occasions before having his first green-out reaction:

> I went to this party, and we had like two ounces [56 grams] of pot. My friend rolled a massive blunt, and three of us shared it. Then he rolled another one—we smoked that and I was feeling pretty unsteady. I forget if we had more joints or went straight to smoking cones, but I hit the bong and started feeling out of my head. I couldn't really move, wanted everyone to get away from me, and felt confused about what was going on around me. I threw up a few times and remember it crossing my mind that I would die. I felt paralysed and trapped in my own body, and honestly couldn't move for all the numbness. A person looking at me might have thought I was asleep, but actually my mind was running at a hundred miles an hour. I didn't move for what felt like forever. What pissed me off so much was that my friend was standing right there watching me saying stuff like, 'You're messed up dude.' It made it so much worse for me. I felt like the experience was never going to end, but when I finally snapped out of it, everything that had been going on around me hit clearly. After this I realized that I'd greened out, and went outside to vomit behind the trees. I've never heaved so hard in my life, I think I nearly threw up a lung. I guess this showed me to never underestimate the effect of THC—sometimes it really sneaks up on you. I kinda got

traumatized from it, getting scared that if I smoked again it would happen again.

How can you help someone who is greening out?

You can help them by reassuring them they are going to be okay and by taking them to a quiet place with fresh air, sitting them in a comfortable position, and giving them a glass of water or something sweet (such as juice or candy). If the person feels so sick that they start to vomit, when they have finished lie them down on their side, not on their back, so they don't choke on their vomit, and keep them in a quiet, safe spot where you can monitor them. If someone is physically sick, it is important that you never leave them on their own, not even for the shortest time. Suffocating on vomit is a very real threat, especially if they have been drinking or using other drugs as well, and can lead to an otherwise unnecessary death. See <http://ncpic.org.au/ncpic/publications/factsheets/article/looking-after-a-friend-on-cannabis>.

If a person is experiencing panic attacks, anxiety or paranoia after using cannabis, most of the time these effects can be managed through reassurance. Try to calm the person down: reassure them that these feelings will pass in time; take them to a safe and quiet place and stay with them; let them know that you are here to help them; and if there is something you can do for them, do it. If they don't calm down, try to distract them with other topics of discussion. If nothing you do is helping, and the person continues to feel bad or their condition gets worse, then it is important to get more help. Call an ambulance or take them to get medical help so that they can be treated quickly and safely.

Many people who green out once say the experience repeats itself if they try to use cannabis again. It is important to bear this in mind when making a decision about whether to use cannabis.

A rare condition called pot paresis is related to greening out (Feldman & Hadfield 2009); this is muscle pain and weakness associated with consuming large amounts of salty and sweet foods after smoking cannabis. Taking in lots of carbohydrates increases insulin levels, which drives potassium into the muscles and drops potassium in the blood to dangerous levels. Anyone experiencing muscle pain and weakness after smoking cannabis and having the munchies should seek urgent medical care.

Myth no. 5: Cannabis and driving—the enhancement myth

> I drive safer when stoned.
> Fifteen miles an hour is safer, right?
>
> —Anonymous

We've all heard the argument or heard about research showing that using cannabis actually *improves* your driving performance—being stoned makes you drive slower, more cautiously and with greater alertness. Unfortunately, the facts about cannabis and driving do not support the argument that driving stoned is safe.

Cannabis slows down your reaction time to the point where slower driving will not compensate for the reduced ability to respond rapidly to a given driving scenario. Road accidents happen with very little warning, and a delayed reaction time will make you much less likely to see one coming with enough time to avoid it. Being stoned can also impair your judgement on the road, making you much more likely to be responsible for a hazard that could lead to a road accident. How do we know this? Research into cannabis and driving is continually growing, with findings pointing in a clear direction. A few years ago, the picture was clouded because the research only looked at cannabis metabolites in the urine of those involved in accidents, and we now know that this does not measure intoxication and hence driving impairment, so the results were meaningless. When looking at research on cannabis and driving, it is important to only consider recent research using blood THC levels. A good review of the current research that is outlined below is provided by Hartman and Huestis (2013).

Laboratory studies have found that, when stoned, people experience several problems likely to negatively affect their driving skills. These include slower rates of tracking objects; poorer attention span and reaction time; worsened hand-eye coordination; and impaired brain function relating to concentration and time estimation. Unsurprisingly, the more stoned a person is, the greater the deficiency in driving skills. Impairments from using cannabis are present for several hours, with the risk of an accident reducing from seven-fold one hour after smoking to just over two-fold two hours after smoking. Driving simulator studies have also identified several ways in which cannabis smoking increases the risk of a road accident, including worsened steering, increased physical effort and discomfort, increased speed variability and decreased reaction times.

Most important, however, is the fact that compromised driving as a result of using cannabis is not just evident in laboratory studies, but also in real life. The risk of being involved in a motor vehicle collision when driving under the influence of cannabis is a bit less than twice that of driving when not stoned. The risk of being involved in a fatal collision is a bit more than twice as likely (Ashbridge, Hayden & Cartwright 2012).

It should be remembered, of course, that cannabis does not just impair driving skills but also all of the tasks that involve similar skills. For this reason, there is workplace drug testing in occupations with higher risk of accidents, such as for those working in mines and anyone operating heavy machinery. For example, police and members of the defence force, who have access to firearms and are required to make highly complex decisions on the run, are also targeted for workplace cannabis and other drug testing.

Clearly, driving under the influence of cannabis is not a good idea, and can even dramatically affect your life if you are unlucky enough to get into a serious accident. One of our research participants, Michael, told us his story about cannabis and driving.

Michael is 29 and recently wrote to us seeking assistance to quit cannabis. When asked about his reasons for quitting, he described the car accident that had triggered his decision. Michael had been smoking cannabis with two friends before they all got in his car to drive over to a party. When switching from the left to the right lane—a task that he would normally describe as simple—Michael hit another car lightly from the side. Panicked, and unable to think in a hurry, he tried to correct his mistake by quickly going back to the left, but hit a second car, this time with high impact. Both cars were badly damaged, and the driver of the second vehicle he hit was injured. Police, paramedics and the fire brigade came. Despite Michael putting on his most convincing 'sobriety face', the police suspected Michael and his friends of being intoxicated. Michael was drug tested and returned a positive result for cannabis use. At the time he wrote to us, he was awaiting trial on multiple charges. He described the accident and what followed as the scariest time of his life, and the decision to drive stoned as the one he most regrets.

As mentioned previously, random roadside drug testing for cannabis uses oral fluid testing followed by blood testing if you prove positive on the initial test. This means you should not drive for a considerable time after smoking—at least six and preferably 24 hours—as there is no individual certainty of metabolism rates. There are now breath tests for cannabis in development that are likely to be the next step in roadside drug tests. For more information and resources, see <http://ncpic.org.au/youngpeople/cannabis-and-driving>.

Myth no. 6: Yes, but it cures cancer doesn't it?

Prior to the development of modern medicine, cannabis was used for medicinal purposes. It enjoyed a brief period of popularity as a medicinal herb in Europe and the United States in the 1800s, being prescribed for various conditions including menstrual cramps, asthma, cough, insomnia, birth labour, migraine, throat infection and withdrawal from opiate use. Because of the problems with titrating a dose, there were issues with patients being given too little or too much, resulting in anything from no effect to adverse effects. Cannabis was removed from the register of medicines in the United States in the early 1900s, and made illegal at around the same time.

Unfortunately, the science on the medicinal potential of cannabis has been hijacked by the pro-cannabis legalisation lobby as a way of increasing the drug's reputation as being a harmless, health-giving herb and establishing retail structures (Sabet 2013). While some involved in the programs in the US where various models of medical cannabis are operating are doing so in good faith, many just wish to increase availability and make money. It is a puzzling system to those outside the United States that people can vote that an untested medicine be available despite there being a very rigorous Food and Drug Administration to ensure the medicines are effective, safe, pure and of known dosage. No other drug in modern medicine is smoked.

While the risks of smoking can be mitigated by preparing cannabis as a range of food products, this introduces new problems. The first is that any cannabis that is eaten has to be metabolised by the liver, which creates a new cannabinoid (11-hydroxy-THC) that is more potent than THC. This means that the onset of the effect is delayed and unpredictable compared with smoked cannabis. While much of the initial THC is lost during the digestion process, the user can end up way more stoned than they intended (as we mentioned earlier in the section on greening out) when the dose eventually takes effect. The second concern is that edible cannabis products—such as brownies, ice cream and pot tarts—are frequently sweet and thus attractive to children. It is much easier for infants and young children to overdose on THC, leading to coma and the need for urgent medical care (Wang, Roosevelt & Heard 2013). This risk also extends to domestic pets with cases of severe illness and death associated with cannabis butter in particular (Fitzgerald, Bronstein & Newquist 2013). In addition, making products highly palatable is a marketing ploy successfully used by the alcohol industry to recruit young drinkers, and is another example of the entrepreneurial nature of the industry.

So what does the science say? Over the past 20 years, there has been increasing international focus on the potential of cannabis as a treatment option for various medical conditions, mainly where traditional first-line drugs have proven ineffective for particular sub-classes of patients. The most common conditions include pain and nausea associated with cancer, HIV, rheumatoid arthritis and peripheral neuropathic pain. Cannabis has also been used to treat the nightmares associated with post-traumatic stress disorder (PTSD) (Fraser 2009). Accordingly, during this time, the amount of pre-clinical and clinical research into the effects of pharmaceutical preparations of cannabis on humans has increased significantly. A recent review of relevant randomised controlled trials of cannabis-based medicines found 38 published trials, of which 71 per cent found some efficacy (Aggarwal 2013). These trials used approved medications rather than smoked herbal cannabis, and found that while beneficial effects were achieved, most trials were only short-term in duration and longer trials were needed in order to comprehensively gauge the therapeutic benefits of cannabinoids.

Potential benefits of cannabinoids

A number of studies using both smoked and pharmaceutical preparations of cannabis have been published over the last 30 years. Some modest success in treating a range of conditions has been reported with this drug class—predominantly in the treatment of the symptoms of multiple sclerosis (MS). Nabiximols has been tested for a number of conditions, other than cannabis dependence, in human trials set in the community, with no evidence of tolerance, significant intoxication or any form of withdrawal syndrome when dosing stopped. (Borgelt et al. 2013). Nabiximols is a botanical preparation comprised of approximately equal parts THC and CBD in an oral spray. It has also been shown to have some success as an adjunctive treatment with patients suffering from brachial plexus avulsion, central neuropathic pain in MS, rheumatoid arthritis, peripheral neuropathic pain and pain associated with advanced cancer (see <https://ncpic.org.au/ncpic/publications/bulletins/article/the-use-of-cannabis-for-medical-purposes>). Various studies in MS patients have shown that at the low doses used, there are no signs of addiction. To date, nabiximols presents the best hope for pharmaceutical cannabinoids as a second- or third-line treatment when the most effective traditional treatments aren't working well enough, or as an additional therapy.

Myth no. 7: . . . and cannabis never killed anyone!

This is the typical *coup de grace* of the potologist or argumentative adolescent, and has been the accepted wisdom on the topic until very recently. Dying is not that simple; there is a difference between dying from an acute overdose of a drug and a drug-related death. Either way, you would not have died if you hadn't taken the drug.

Cannabis is similar to stimulants such as cocaine and methamphetamine in that it does not suppress breathing like heroin and alcohol, so you don't die directly from the effects of the drug in a dose-related manner. With depressants such as alcohol and heroin, your level of consciousness reduces as you take more, until your brain is no longer able to protect your airways if you vomit or are badly positioned and the stimulus to breath is suppressed. This is a direct and predictable drug effect that is influenced by general health, how experienced the person is with the drug and their level of tolerance, and the use of other drugs at the same time that have the same effect. These combinations are typically alcohol with benzodiazepines such as Valium and opioids such as heroin or codeine.

It is often suggested that humans simply cannot get enough THC into their system to die from its direct effects, but unfortunately this is not the same as saying you can't die as a result of using cannabis. The British Royal College of Pathologists included cannabis in the drug toxicity listing of causes of sudden cardiac death in 2002. This was based on a study that used a sophisticated design to show that smoking cannabis increases the risk of having a heart attack (myocardial infarction) by almost five-fold (4.8) in the first hour after smoking compared with periods of non-use and 1.7 times in the second hour (Mittleman et al. 2001). This is consistent with the known effects of THC on heart rate (increases), blood pressure (increases), oxygen uptake in the blood (reduces) and contraction of blood vessels, including to the heart muscle (ischaemia) (Cadet, Bisagno & Milroy 2014).

Over the years, there have been a number of cases in the literature that reported cannabis as a primary or secondary cause of death, usually associated with a heart attack or stroke. There is often dispute about the actual role of cannabis in these deaths, as complete post-mortems or full pathology results are not usually available. A recent report of a 21-year-old university student who was undergoing a 24-hour routine heart monitor test noted that his heart stopped beating (asystole) for up to 5.8 seconds when he inhaled cannabis (Menahem 2013). This was suggested as one of the possible mechanisms of sudden death.

The best documented deaths associated with cannabis use were reported in Germany. Two pathologists wrote a paper that very thoroughly investigated all aspects of the unexpected deaths of two, young, thought to be healthy men who were under the influence of cannabis. This even included genetic studies along with full post-mortems and toxicological and tissue examinations. No other cause of death was found, except for an enlarged heart in one of the men (Hartung et al. 2014). The paper concluded that the young men experienced fatal cardiovascular complications from smoking cannabis.

Once again, the potologists were up in arms and cried that this was only a diagnosis of exclusion rather than actual proof of the cause of death (as with other drug-related deaths) and that cannabis smoking is safer than straining to go to the toilet in terms of risk of a cardiac-related death (*Mixmag* 2014). The difference is that constipation may be difficult to avoid, but smoking cannabis definitely is not!

CHAPTER 4

Does cannabis affect your mental health?

Even more controversial than the physical and public health effects of cannabis is its influence on mental health. Psychosis and schizophrenia are the most commonly noted community concerns about cannabis use, particularly among young people. Depression and anxiety, however, are far more common mental health problems.

Chicken or egg?

The perennial question is whether cannabis use causes depression, being depressed makes you use cannabis, or something else in your life is causing you to be a depressed cannabis user. There are multiple candidates as mediators in the association between cannabis use and anxiety and other mental health conditions. These include the role of adolescent brain development changes in general (Spear 2013) and the endocannabinoid system in particular (Rubino, Zamberletti & Parolaro 2012), trauma such as childhood maltreatment, length of exposure to cannabis and age of first cannabis exposure.

The issue of whether or not the relationship between cannabis use and mental health is influenced by genes is also the subject of a growing literature–typically concerning abuse and dependence symptomatology. Twin studies have reported that the rates of other drug use disorders and common psychiatric conditions are highly correlated with the extent of cannabis involvement. There is consistent evidence of the influence of genetic heritage on a range of cannabis-related behaviours, such as the early opportunity to use (at or before 15 years of age), early initiation of use (at or before 16 years of age), using more frequently and developing cannabis use disorders (including addiction) (Lynskey et al. 2012).

The evidence of the role of cannabis in the development and course of the most common mental health conditions' differs, and needs to be explored separately.

Does cannabis help depression?

It is more usual that the family and friends of those with cannabis related mental health problems are the first to reach out for information and support, rather than the person swept up in the experience. Our free telephone helpline recently received a call from Tara, who was concerned about her husband's depression and use of cannabis. Tara described her husband as having chronic depression, which had strongly impacted on both of them for many years. As a result of her husband's depression, the business they owned together and their family life had been suffering, and Tara was at a loss to know what she could do. Her husband was a daily cannabis user, and refused to give up as he believed that cannabis was the only thing that offered him any relief from the depression. Tara did notice that her husband appeared noticeably happier in the evenings while he was stoned. But the next morning he would always be lethargic and uncommunicative, and would seem to be more depressed than ever. Tara wondered whether cannabis really was helping her husband to manage the depression or whether it could actually be the source of his problem.

Tara's dilemma is a difficult one because the inter-action between cannabis use and depression can seem complex, especially to the user. Many people say one of the reasons they use cannabis is that in the short term it can greatly improve their mood. For Tara's husband, cannabis offered immediate relief from his depression, as it put him in a different mindset that made him less focused on his feelings of hopelessness despite not actually lifting his mood. But there is evidence that smoking cannabis may make depression worse. People who use cannabis have been shown to have higher levels of depression and depressive symptoms than those who do not use cannabis. Young women appear to be more likely to experience depression as a result of their cannabis use. People who start smoking cannabis at a younger age (early adoles-cence) and smoke heavily are more likely to experience negative consequences. This may, in turn, lead to mental health problems, but may also lead to more general life problems, like conflict at home or school/work, financial problems and memory problems. If someone has a genetic vulnerability—such as a close family member with depression—or has an existing mental health issue, they should avoid using cannabis.

One important question about the co-occurrence of depression and cannabis use relates to which comes first. After all, it seems just as likely that people who are already depressed would turn to cannabis to lift their mood as it does that people who use cannabis will become depressed as a result of their use. The research on this issue does give reason to believe that using cannabis can lead to or worsen depression. For example, a recent review of studies looking at cannabis use and the later onset of depression showed that non-depressed people who used cannabis weekly or more often were 62 per cent more likely to develop depression later on than non-depressed people who didn't use cannabis (Lev-Ran et al. 2013).

If you are using cannabis and also experiencing depression, your family doctor can refer you to drug and alcohol services and/or mental health services. Ideally, they will tackle both issues at the same time. Treatment usually involves counselling, and in some cases medicine is prescribed to assist with symptoms of mental health problems while helping you stop your cannabis use.

Suicide

In developed countries, suicide is now the second leading cause of death among 10-24-year-olds, so any preventable risk factor is potentially of great public health importance. A growing number of studies by health statisticians and economists identify cannabis use as an important risk factor for suicidal behaviours. Genetic studies have also identified the role of cannabis dependence in the increased risk (in the order of 2.5 to 2.9 times) of suicidal thoughts and attempts (Lynskey et al. 2004). The same study also reported that those who started using cannabis prior to the age of 17 had elevated rates of subsequent suicide attempts (of around 3.5 times).

An important study on this question investigated whether regular cannabis use leads to the onset of suicidal ideation or the reverse (feeling suicidal drives you to smoke cannabis). Using information from a New Zealand study that followed babies from birth for the next 30 years, the researchers were able to control for all known other characteristics of the individual, their parents and the socio-economic background of the family that might also be causing the association. They found that cannabis use at the intensity of several times per week led to higher rates of developing suicidal thoughts—but only among males. They did not find any evidence for the suggestion that it might be thoughts of wanting to commit suicide that had led to cannabis use for either gender (Van Ours et al. 2012).

Does cannabis relax you and help anxiety?

The link between cannabis and anxiety is confusing because cannabis is often used to relieve symptoms of anxiety. In fact, when people who use cannabis regularly are asked why they use, one of the most common responses is to relieve stress and anxiety. Although some people say the use of cannabis alleviates their symptoms of anxiety, there is evidence that smoking cannabis may make anxiety worse, and may even trigger the development of an anxiety disorder.

The experience of Lee, who had started experiencing intense anxiety immediately after smoking cannabis, is a good example. Lee had been smoking for around seven years, since she was about 17. Her usage level had varied from occasional before she left school up to heavy (lots every day) once she got her own apartment. Smoking cannabis had never caused her problems, until recently when she said that smoking was making her feel light-headed, followed by a racing heart, and then feelings of intense anxiety and panic. These feelings would carry on until she sobered up, and ruin her evening every time she smoked. Lee said she had all but stopped smoking, apart from the occasional couple of puffs here and there. When she tried to smoke any more than this, the anxiety would inevitably come back again, regardless of how relaxed and safe the setting she was in felt. Lee described herself as always having been a bit of a worrier, but smoking cannabis had been her sure-fire way to relax. She wondered whether it was possible to reach a point where it was necessary to quit smoking cannabis. Could this be happening because she had smoked so much cannabis in the past? Had she overdone it to the point of no return?

Lee posted about her problem on a chat site for cannabis users. Unfortunately, responses and advice about her issue generally added to her confusion. These included pieces of advice such as, 'I went through something similar to what you're going through now about ten years into my smoking career. I resolved the problem through meditation', as well as dismissal of the issue: 'No one has ever died from marijuana . . . you're completely safe.' However, many more people came forward to say that they had experienced the same thing. Some also said that their anxiety was now present even when they weren't stoned.

So what does the evidence say about cannabis and anxiety? Studies have shown that cannabis use can lead to symptoms of anxiety—such as panic—in the short term. One-fifth of cannabis users experience these kinds of immediate effects of cannabis intoxication (see <http://ncpic.org.au/ncpic/publications/factsheets/article/cannabis-and-mental-health>). While there is little doubt that cannabis use can cause anxiety, there is mixed evidence on whether it leads to an anxiety disorder that persists even when use has ceased (Crippa et al. 2009).

If you use cannabis on a regular basis and you are starting to notice increases in your anxiety when stoned, or you are just noticing increases in your stress and anxiety overall, it might be useful to consider the possibility that cannabis is contributing to the problem. After a period of cutting back or quitting, you might start to notice positive differences in your mood, including less stress.

Cannabis and psychosis: Reefer madness?

This highly contested debate preoccupies many scientists and bloggers. Some strongly argue that, as cannabis use has increased over the past couple of decades but the rates of diagnosed schizophrenia generally have not, the two cannot be directly linked. As there is no mental health condition with a 100 per cent genetic cause, this is obviously a truism. It needs to be remembered that doctors and scientists don't definitely know what causes schizophrenia, so we can't be sure that while cannabis use is exerting its influence, other risk factors may have reduced, keeping the incidence steady. Overall, it is estimated that 8-14 per cent of psychosis cases could be avoided with no cannabis use in the community (Kuepper et al. 2011).

First, what is schizophrenia? It is a brain disorder that affects the way a person acts, thinks and sees the world. People with schizophrenia have an altered perception of reality, and often a significant loss of contact with the real world. They may see or hear things that don't exist, speak in strange or confusing ways, believe that others are trying to harm them or feel like they're being constantly watched. With such a blurred line between the real and the imaginary, schizophrenia makes it difficult—even frightening—to negotiate the activities of daily life (see <www.helpguide. org/mental/schizophrenia_symptom.htm>). Schizophrenia is a psychotic disorder, but people can experience psychotic symptoms in other disorders such as bipolar affective disorder and other conditions. While we don't clearly know what causes schizophrenia, some risk factors have been identified. It has a strong hereditary component, but the disorder is only influenced by genetics, not determined by it. While schizophrenia runs in families, about 60 per cent of those with schizophrenia have no family members with the disorder. As for the environmental factors involved, more and more research is pointing to stress as a cause, either during pregnancy or at a later stage of development. The kinds of stress that have been identified include exposure to a viral infection during pregnancy, low oxygen levels during birth (from prolonged labour or premature birth), a virus during infancy, early parental loss or separation, physical or sexual abuse in childhood, migration and living in a stressful city environment (Heinz, Deserno & Reininghaus 2013). One of the easily avoidable environmental factors associated with schizophrenia is cannabis use (Isaac, Isaac & Holloway 2005).

It is well established in laboratory studies that THC can produce psychotic symptoms in otherwise normal individuals during, and sometimes shortly after, intoxication (Morrison et al 2009). Surveys of cannabis users also reveal that experiencing psychotic-like symptoms when smoking cannabis is not uncommon, with one study reporting that one in seven cannabis users (14 per cent) reported 'strange, unpleasant experiences such as hearing voices' or 'becoming convinced that someone is trying to harm you' after using cannabis (Thomas 1996). It is certainly true that some people diagnosed with a psychotic illness believe that cannabis was the cause. Mary's story of using cannabis and her subsequent experiences of psychotic symptoms is an example.

Mary was diagnosed with drug-induced psychosis after smoking around 20 cannabis joints a day every day for six years during late high school and university. She described experiencing a variety of symptoms of psychosis. These included delusions, such as the belief that she could control other people's minds and that her thoughts could influence the mood of an entire room full of people. She also believed that people were putting poison into her food and doing things to deliberately drive her mad. She described often hearing voices that would give a running commentary on her actions, as well as seeing her mother's face in paint patches on the wall and having long conversations with her. After seeing a university counsellor about these issues, Mary was referred to a mental health hospital ward, where she was diagnosed with schizoaffective disorder. She subsequently quit smoking cannabis, but still suffers the same symptoms seven years later, despite being on various anti-psychotic medications. In addition, she often feels suicidal. Mary believes that cannabis 'created strange and unreal paths inside my mind', and blames cannabis for the 'living nightmare' she believes her life has become.

To summarise the very complex evidence, cannabis use may precipitate schizophrenia in people who are vulnerable due to genetic or environmental risk factors. New research also suggests that cannabis use in those who have these vulnerabilities increases the chances of experiencing psychotic symptoms. In other words, its use appears to induce psychosis in people who might otherwise have remained well (Burns 2013). Whatever the type of study examined, cannabis use is associated with about a doubling of the risk of developing a psychotic illness like schizophrenia.

The age of onset of psychotic illness among cannabis users is almost three years younger than among non-users (Large et al. 2011). Cannabis use may also decrease the age of onset of the early (prodromal) symptoms, which may reduce even further the window of normal psychosocial and vocational development prior to the onset of debilitating symptoms.

The media use headlines such as 'cannabis cures psychosis'. This is both confusing and misleading. It arises because cannabidiol (CBD) is known to have anti-psychotic effects in humans and animals. As already discussed, cannabis today has almost no CBD in it, so smoking this kind of cannabis will definitely not cure anything, let alone schizophrenia. Studies exploring the impact of pure, pharmaceutical-grade CBD on schizophrenia, however, are definitely warranted (Deiana 2012).

In addition to the onset of schizophrenia, cannabis use is associated with poorer medication compliance among people using medication for psychosis (Zammit et al., 2008). Further, continued cannabis use frequently leads to poorer treatment outcomes over and above those related to medication non-compliance. Clausen et al. (2014) recently showed that, after ruling out the effects of insufficient anti-psychotic treatment and the way the patient was faring at the outset of the study, those who continued using cannabis after commencing treatment for psychosis had greater psychotic symptoms and poorer social functioning five years later than patients who didn't use cannabis or who had stopped using it after their psychosis symptoms first appeared. In summary, research suggests that cannabis use is associated with an increased risk of psychotic symptoms and disorders. This risk is greater for people who have risk factors, and especially those who are already experiencing sub-clinical psychotic symptoms.

Further, cannabis use is associated with a younger age of onset of psychosis. A study that pooled the best quality research looking at age of onset of psychosis among those who were cannabis users and those who did not use cannabis found that, on average, the cannabis users were 2.7 years younger when they had their first episode (Large et al. 2011). Interestingly, tobacco use had no influence on the age of psychosis onset. In addition to preventing some episodes of psychotic illness, delaying an inevitable episode would allow the sufferer a further two to three years of psychosis-free functioning to further their educational and social relationships, which would in turn reduce the level of disability associated with their illness.

Once someone has begun experiencing psychosis, continuing to use cannabis reduces the likelihood that they will comply with medication regimes, and increases the risk of greater symptom severity and worse social outcomes. It is encouraging that the evidence suggests that once cannabis is no longer used, the nature and severity of symptoms and level of functioning are no different than for those with the same psychotic illnesses who never used cannabis.

There are very few areas where academics are willing to give black and white advice, but for those with schizophrenia or other psychotic disorders, cannabis is definitely not the drug for you.

CHAPTER 5

But it isn't addictive . . . is it?

In the mid-1990s, when we started working on the question of whether or not there was a dependence syndrome associated with cannabis use, the scientific evidence from animal and human studies was growing but many were sceptical about whether it could be true. Some prominent medical colleagues attacked us in the media and dismissed cannabis use as akin to chocolate addiction. While the scientists are now agreed that there are physical and psychological dimensions to cannabis dependence, the sceptics are screaming even louder.

Before taking you on a quick tour of the scientific literature on cannabis dependence, explaining how dependence and addiction are the same thing, and what it means to be addicted, the story of someone deeply involved in cannabis use and politics will explain what it means more clearly than a bunch of scientific studies possibly could.

We received a letter in 1999 from Bob, who has approved the reproduction of his words. The letter was in response to an article in a local newspaper, where we were commenting that cannabis addiction problems were treatable. He is a well-known cannabis activist from Nimbin in Northern New South Wales. Nimbin is the Australian epicentre of 'hippiedom', an area akin to Humboldt County in California or Christiania in Denmark, both of which started out primarily as areas of counter-cultural experimentation but subsequently became better known as regions associated with cannabis production and/or trafficking. Here is Bob's letter:

> I have been a daily user of cannabis over the last 26 years (I was 26 years old at the time I got started) since I was seduced by its allure after using it one night after a national conference of social studies students. A random moment, 'try this', which had huge and unforeseeable consequences for me. Overnight I became 'hooked' and its use became central to my life and whatever meaning I put upon existence from that point on.
>
> In retrospect I was at the time a reasonably muddled, naive, extremely shy and reticent, though earnest and well-meaning, young man and there was the immediate sense that this was the feeling of wellbeing that I had been seeking my whole life: a sense of confidence, cohesion and ease with life as it was occurring and unfolding around me. Within a short period I was using regularly including times when I was confronted with difficult and trying episodes such as in personal conflicts or at work, despite at times thinking I was going to die as a consequence of its use—perhaps they were 'overdoses' but I think it was just an indication of how strong and unpredictable a substance cannabis is. These situations

resulted in my becoming extremely disoriented, paranoid, emotionally and physically overloaded, etc. Despite these scary experiences I rarely wavered from immediately going back for more.

I had always been something of a hippie but a political, ethical hippie given more to healthy living, political and social justice activities and visions of a simple life rather than the hedonistic hippiedom that the media publicise. I'd tried pot a number of times earlier in my life but apart from a mild sense of hilarity, I'd never really got stoned as I was to experience it that night in Sydney. Ironically I had quit cigarette smoking 2 years before and was feeling wonderfully healthy and was actively exploring the new wave of humanistic or popular psychology going at the time.

From that point of time on it came to be central to my life. My wife wasn't happy about the change in me and observed that it made me 'cocky' (overly and arrogantly confident) but I enjoyed the feeling. It made the intolerable times tolerable, although without changing the circumstances that caused the sense of intolerableness. It was like my ego got bolstered in much the same way as the alcoholic describes it when he/she is everyone's mate, and which for this shy and nervous kid was an illumination and sense of personal liberation.

As I had children I determined not to deprive them financially as a consequence of my burgeoning habit and so I moved away to rural lifestyles where, amongst other things, I could grow my own supply and avoid the pitfalls of a predatory market situation.

Bob goes on to describe how he moved to Nimbin, where cannabis use was very widely accepted, in 1980. He stayed there until a year before he wrote the letter:

> For the pot-smoking hippie, Nimbin was antithetical to anywhere else I'd lived; it was a community of oddball freaks with an apparent majority of new settlers (from professionals to the street people) using cannabis as a preferred substance of intoxication and its use was relatively open and accepted, even when not being used, most everywhere. Being in Nimbin allowed me to indulge in my dreams for a better, more just and tolerant society though in retrospect all the while in a befuddled, stoned state.
>
> Because I attributed to cannabis an almost mystical healing quality I felt that it was demeaning to its spiritual attributes to sell, traffic in it, and especially to profit from its sale to dependent users caught in its [web], despite that being a big part of the local economy. Sadly the more time that is spent living largely in an illegal environment, the more illegality becomes infatuating and corrupting, not to mention greed inducing. Despite my high idealism eventually I too occasionally offered up some of my stash for sale (though in my defence always on a pretty small scale and mostly to support my anti-drug law activities) but I never felt easy about this as not only did it seem like I was corrupting its 'integrity', I had also had insights into what I perceived was a deleterious side of its use which continually nagged away at me, though as before I still couldn't bring myself to quit.
>
> Police activity in Nimbin tended to be pretty cowboy-like and I was amazed and disconcerted by the degree of

fear, suspicion and paranoia that existed within the local counter-culture community. In 1988 I commenced what was for years a one-person campaign aimed at the repeal of the drug laws, which I figured would remove much of the deleterious effects associated with its use. Because I had no money and no social position worth considering, I relied on outrageousness and political theatre to make an impact. Right from the start I realised that I could not encourage the use of pot but in hindsight I see that pot promotion was what I [was] perceived to be doing by others. I agitated tirelessly in the local area and I stood as a candidate in the state elections of 1995 and 1999. I smoked a much publicised joint on the steps of the Nimbin police station and came to be considered something of a local outlaw identity. Later, when I attracted 'followers' and generated a hometown movement, I realised that the majority of those I'd recruited were people who were into evangelising the use of pot and defending the trade in cannabis which I felt was blighting the town, corrupting the general (as opposed to the official) population and internally destroying the aspirations of the counter-culture. But by then things had taken on a life of their own and were getting wildly out of my control.

Allied with this was the growing sense that cannabis wasn't the universal panacea that I considered it might be for me. The problem was that being stoned every day from first thing in the morning (I was at least a 20+ joint a day user) meant I couldn't objectively ascertain what was going on. I largely rationalised my use of cannabis as self-medicating an almost crippling depression and sense of despair, but I was becoming unsure whether the pot cured or caused the depression. Various young people in the area were reportedly suffering the consequences of their youthful use. Personally I was also becoming a person much given to extreme mood swings that included volatile outbursts of anger (so much for the peaceful spaced out hippie!). I'd tried on and off for the last few years to try and give up using cannabis but I always reverted back.

He goes on to talk about the effect cannabis use was having on Nimbin, including an out-of-control drug market that included injectable drugs financed by the sale of cannabis. The use of alcohol and other substances, and gambling, were also big problems. Given the peace-and-love hippie reputation, he was saddened by the anti-social and daily violent behaviour and disrespect on the streets in the town. In 1997 he quit the pro-cannabis organisation he had founded and become a public critic of what Nimbin had become. Reflecting on his personal life, he talked of the breakdown of two relationships which he attributed in large part to his cannabis use. He knew he needed to make a change in his life, and decided to quit cannabis. He felt this required a move to Sydney in order to remove himself from the pot-centred life in Nimbin; he decided to devote his life to working with homeless people and with an organisation that gave advice and information to families affected by alcohol and other drugs. He goes on to talk about that experience:

Next week will be 3 months for me without smoking or using cannabis. This is the longest I've been without using pot in 26 years. Although it's only early days I've observed that I don't have anywhere near the same amount of mood swings and virtually none of the anger. My bouts of depression have diminished enormously and when one does hit, it doesn't last as long or affect me as profoundly. I seem to be able to move on from where I am and not get too stuck. But it's been a lonely path. I've had no support, no support groups, and had to rely totally on my own strength of vision, and when emotional crises have hit I've had to work hard to avoid reverting back to a joint as a lock-stepped response to dealing with stress. But I've done it.

My experience has shown me that there is a state of addiction and dependence for users such as myself to contend with despite all protestations by the cannabis lobby (myself included, I need to say) to the contrary and that for people wishing to toss that deceptively difficult habituation there's no clear or easily available roadmap out there to follow or to chart one's progress. It worries me that there is so much misinformation peddled about how cannabis can make one a better, more sensitive, religious person and a downplaying of the difficulties associated with quitting or modifying pot use, as well as a denial of the potential dangers involved with its use. Many people, professionals even, minimise the downsides of pot and this, I think, is to a large part responsible for the high rates of use uptake being recorded by young people. My own role in helping make pot seem 'cool' or 'hip' is the cause of much regret to me.

He concludes the letter by offering to assist us in our research and asking for any material we developed to help people quit:

It is sad that 15 years later very little has changed, drugwise, for the better in Nimbin: on the contrary the town has become a tourist destination driven to a large extent by the predominance of the promotion and availability of cannabis. For most of that period I've attempted to keep myself sober from cannabis. I backslide from time to time when I come into contact with dear friends who use cannabis, so my sobriety has been helped by my not keeping company with other users. I do however miss the sense of community I shared in Nimbin and for me it's often a lonely long haul. But there is life after cannabis. I run and swim, I meditate, read a lot and I play my ukulele, and the highs I get from these activities are of a purer and sweeter kind than I ever got from being stoned. And I know now I can stop after the binge, though I can't let myself go for long using. The occasional use reveals to me still how strong the substance is and how much I am affected. I stumble, both physically and vocally. I can become either a garrulous self-obsessed extrovert or a socially inept and awkward isolate. Neither lasts or gives satisfaction.

I presume there are self-help groups out there but I see very little evidence of such. Self-help is vital in my estimation as users need to empower themselves. As a general rule cannabis use (and users) are a hidden but thriving sub-group everywhere in our society but rarely acknowledged. Generally they are publicly challenged only by the more extreme anti-drug zealots which diminishes the credibility of most such messages. Most people conveniently shrug off or are prepared to ignore drug use in society until sadly a crisis occurs with a family member developing negative consequences of use and then the family are left mostly alone in trying to keep things together. My heart aches for people caught in this situation.

Bob's story highlights many of the themes that come up when regular cannabis users move into addiction. While many treatment providers talk disparagingly to those seeking help about their denial of their problems with cannabis, it is really a rational defence to a perceived attack on one's character, morals and personal failings. Giving a drug mystical or special powers is part of this process for many, as they begin to lose control over their use of the drug. The suggestion that you could be addicted is usually somewhere between annoying and horrifying. In addition to the natural inclination to dismiss such a suggestion, in the case of cannabis there is a genuine ignorance among some users who have only been exposed to the culture of cannabis as a harmless herb unlike the other bad drugs, like alcohol and tobacco.

We recently had a paper published on a study that investigated the use of a drug in the management of cannabis withdrawal. The paper was published on a website called Science Alert, and the following are some examples of the kinds of comments (with no corrections) that were posted from the 'no way', to 'maybe' to 'yes sure' positions:

What nonsense, cannabis doesn't cause physical dependence (unlike tobacco, alcohol, and caffeine).

That's crazy, I never herd of such a thing as withdrawal symptoms or addiction period when it comes to dank. Rediculous. Bu then again, everybodys different and may, just maybe there is such a thing. However, I never heard of such a thing.

I've seen plenty of dependent pot users. I was dependent when I was in my teens. I know people that smoke everyday and can't stop. They live their lives stoned and see stopping as almost impossible to fathom.

It can be very difficult to talk to someone about their problems with cannabis if they aren't aware that it is possible to become addicted. We frequently have to help people recognise that they are not alone with this problem. When they believe they must be the only people struggling to control their use, they have strong feelings of isolation and of being a unique failure in some way compared with all those who argue addiction isn't possible, as they've been using for years and can stop any time they choose to.

To put this discussion in context, it is important to reiterate that, typically, people who use cannabis do not progress to using the drug regularly, or for long periods of time. Most will experiment every now and then during adolescence and early adulthood, and stop using once they are in their mid- to late twenties. However, some people will use cannabis for longer and more often, and become dependent on the drug. The earlier a person starts using cannabis, and the more they use, the more likely they are to become dependent. Studies have shown that males are more likely than females to become dependent on cannabis, simply because they are more likely to use the drug.

The following section briefly explores cannabis addiction and how it is defined and measured.

How is cannabis addiction diagnosed?

This section, along with the next two sections on terminology and diagnoses, is dedicated to the potologists. We realise it is of limited general interest but, given the level of misunderstanding on this issue, we thought it important to include this information.

Relatively little is known about the natural history of cannabis dependence. The onset of dependence most commonly occurs in adolescence or young adulthood, within ten years of initiation (Anthony 2006). Some research has documented the onset of clinical symptoms, commencing with behaviours that indicate a loss of control and continued use despite harm, with withdrawal experienced at a later stage by relatively fewer users (Rosenberg & Anthony 2001).

As with all other mental health conditions, including schizophrenia, cannabis use disorders are diagnosed by interview with a psychologist or psychiatrist. There are two main guiding systems for health professionals to use. The one used most commonly in the research literature on addiction and by health professionals in North America and Australasia is the *Diagnostic and Statistical Manual of Mental Disorders* (American Psychiatric Association 2013). The latest version is commonly referred to as the DSM-5 or DSM-V, and is the American Psychiatric Association's gold standard text on the names, symptoms and diagnostic features of every recognised mental illness, including addictions. The DSM-5 also refers to the codes from the International Classification of Diseases (ICD) to allow clinicians to code for specific mental disorders. The ICD is the official system of the World Health Organization (WHO), to assign codes to diagnoses for insurance claims and other research and public-health purposes (WHO 2010). These codes change quite frequently, so the DSM-5 is preferred because it is more stable and detailed with regard to the addictions; hence it will be our standard in this chapter.

The DSM-5 recognises substance-related disorders resulting from the use of a number of drug classes: alcohol, caffeine, cannabis, hallucinogens of two different classes, inhalants, opioids, sedatives, hypnotics, anxiolytics, stimulants (including amphetamine-type substances, cocaine, and other stimulants), tobacco, and other or unknown substances. It explains that activation of the brain's reward system is central to problems arising from drug use. As discussed earlier, while the pharmacological mechanisms for each drug are different, the activation of the reward system is similar across substances in producing feelings of pleasure or euphoria. The DSM-5 also recognises that people are not all automatically or equally vulnerable to developing substance-related disorders. It is argued that some individuals have lower levels of self-control, which may be related to their genetic or physiological makeup, predisposing them to developing problems if exposed to drugs.

There are two groups of substance-related disorders in the DSM-5: substance-use disorders and substance-induced disorders. Substance-use disorders are patterns of symptoms resulting from use of a substance that the individual continues to take, despite experiencing problems as a result. Substance-induced disorders include intoxication, withdrawal and substance-induced mental disorders, such as psychosis.

What's in a name: Addiction or dependence?

It is hardly surprising that many of us are confused about whether these terms mean the same thing or not, as the professionals in the field keep changing their minds. The term used historically is 'addiction', and its origins are described in an article by Maddux and Desmond (2000). In 1964, the World Health Organization Committee on Addiction-Producing Drugs recommended use of the term 'dependence' in place of 'drug addiction and habituation' (which was seen as a less serious disorder with no physical symptoms). Drug dependence at that time was defined as a state arising from repeated administration of a drug on a periodic or continuous basis. This term was subsequently adopted in the second version of the DSM and eighth version of the ICD system. Since that time, there have been various attempts to have 'addiction' accepted again, as it is considered a behavioural term, whereas 'dependence' is often seen as being confined to physical dependence, as manifested in tolerance (described on p. 76) and withdrawal. The concept of loss of (or impaired) control over use in the term 'addiction' has been central to the understanding of the process the individual is experiencing when seeking treatment.

In 2006, influential US academics were calling for the return of the term 'addiction' in the DSM-5 (O'Brien, Volkow & Li 2006). There was resistance, however, as the term was seen as pejorative when applied to the individual as an addict. A number of medical practitioners had concerns because physical dependence is often seen with other drugs such as anti-depressants, where withdrawal symptoms are experienced when the medication is abruptly stopped, but there is not the same craving that is associated with drugs such as alcohol, cannabis and opioids. There was concern that physicians would see that their patients had physical dependence on a drug and feel they needed to discontinue its use because of addiction when this deprived the patient of an effective medication. While the DSM-5 talks about addictive disorders, the largest change is that it has abandoned the notion of cannabis (or any other drug) abuse, and placed all symptoms in the one category called 'cannabis use disorder'.

DSM-5 criteria for cannabis use disorder diagnosis

Cannabis use disorders span a wide variety of problems arising from use, and cover eleven different criteria:

- *Taking cannabis in larger amounts or for longer than you meant to.* Just as a social drinker can have a glass of wine with dinner and stop, while an alcoholic won't stop until they run out of alcohol or fall asleep, the same is true with cannabis. The person might plan on having a couple of cones then end up having a session that lasts all night. This is not merely a once off event, but a regular occurrence where frequent personal commitments to just have a little are not able to be delivered.
- *Wanting to cut down or stop using cannabis but not managing to.* Many of those who seek assistance to manage their cannabis use have tried many times to quit on their own. While experience of withdrawal symptoms (discussed in Chapter 6) is often what drives them back to use, it is the craving and feelings of compulsion to use

that are the most difficult to manage. It is this impaired control over use that is the hallmark of addiction.

♦ *Spending a lot of time getting, using or recovering from use of cannabis.* Those who meet the diagnostic criteria for a cannabis use disorder typically use cannabis every day. Maintaining this level of use often means that the person is spending a significant proportion of their day getting cannabis, smoking cannabis and, if use is not recommenced soon after waking, recovering from the effects.

♦ *Cravings and urges to use cannabis.* These feelings are the core of the behavioural symptoms of the syndrome that hallmark the loss of control over use.

♦ *Not managing to do what you should at work, home or school, because of cannabis use.* Loss of control is, of course, a subjective thing, but one way to recognise its role in addiction is to reflect on any occasions when you have not made it to work or school because of your cannabis use. Even when making it to work or school most of the time, the effects of cannabis mean that school performance is deteriorating or your career is not going as well as before. Not managing to do what you should at home leads on to the next criterion.

♦ *Continuing to use, even when it causes problems in relationships.* This also extends to your family and other relationships, where you have not met your obligations to those closest to you. It is not just failure to turn up to school, social or professional events but also the loneliness and disappointment of having a partner or even parent who is not emotionally available as they are frequently stoned and in their own world. An additional burden on relationships is the financial cost of cannabis use and its impact on family budgets.

- *Giving up important social, occupational or recreational activities because of cannabis use.* Similar to not managing to do what you should at work, home or school, giving up important activities because of cannabis is more about placing greater priority on cannabis use than on the range of activities that were previously found to be engaging. This includes hobbies, exercise or social activities—particularly going out with non-cannabis-using friends—or memberships of clubs or other organised team activities.

- *Using cannabis again and again, even when it puts you in danger.* While the person may objectively understand that driving or operating heavy machinery when stoned is dangerous, they ignore this knowledge and continue to do these things. Once again, this is an attempt to objectively assess where cannabis use is causing risk to the person and potentially to the community.

- *Continuing to use, even when you know you have a physical or psychological problem that could have been caused or made worse by the substance.* As noted in Chapter 4, continuing to use cannabis when you know it worsens your psychosis or respiratory health is a marker that use is out of control.

- *Needing more of the substance to get the effect you want (tolerance).* Laboratory studies have shown that the development of tolerance to cannabinoids is particularly rapid, and an important decrease in the immediate response has been seen after the second time of use (Maldonado et al. 2011). People develop tolerance in different ways, depending on the type of effect or behaviour being studied, but regular, heavy cannabis users complain that they find it increasingly difficult to get stoned and seek out very high-potency THC preparations. There are many blog posts on this topic—here is an example:

So the first thirty or so times I lit up, I was about 18-20 yrs old, and it was so great: extremely intense, classic noise amplification, time dilation etc. Now I've been smoking about twice a week on average for two or three years. But after getting high regularly, it doesn't do anything much for me. Instead, I get closed eye visuals, weird sinus headaches and real paranoia (like I think people in the room are implying things about me, or that they know things about me, or that they are government agents.) But no real buzz. No munchies, no time dilation, no real sound enhancement, although I do hear voices if I smoke enough. I'm getting good stuff sometimes, and middies. I smoke large and small amounts, often alone. Even when I've stopped smoking a couple of times for a month or so for drug tests, I come back to it and it's the same lack of buzz. I feel like I haven't been really high in years. Does anyone else have a similar experience? (<http://forum.grasscity.com/apprentice-tokers/501095-i-cant-get-high-anymore.html>)

- *Development of withdrawal symptoms, which can be relieved by taking more of the substance.* Chapter 6 explains in detail the nature of cannabis withdrawal.

The DSM-5 allows clinicians to specify how severe the cannabis use disorder is, depending on how many symptoms are identified within the same twelve-month period. Two or three symptoms indicate a mild cannabis use disorder, four or five symptoms indicate a moderate cannabis use disorder and six or more symptoms indicate a severe cannabis use disorder. The previous version, known as the DSM-4-TR required three symptoms to be met in the previous twelve months to meet criteria for cannabis dependence, but only included seven criteria, omitting craving; not being able to do what you should at work, home or school; using cannabis again and again, even when it puts you in danger; and continuing to use, even when it causes problems in relationships. These four were the cannabis abuse criteria in that version of the DSM. Legal issues as a result of cannabis use are no longer included in the DSM-5.

What is the evidence for cannabis addiction?

In Chapter 1 we discussed how our body deals with cannabis, including the CB1 receptors in our brain shown to have specific involvement in the addictive properties of cannabis (see page 7). The neurotransmitters (brain messenger chemicals) involved in the addictive effects of other drugs such as alcohol and opioids are also involved in cannabis addiction. Manipulation of the chemicals and brain reward pathways in laboratory animals has objectively demonstrated models of cannabis tolerance, withdrawal and drug-seeking (Maldonado et al. 2011). The types of studies that examine the rewarding effects of cannabis in animals are very technical, and include techniques that assess whether the drug effects can be detected and influence behaviour, and whether animals will self-administer the drug directly to their brain (see Maladondo et al. 2011 for more details). Interestingly, unlike most other drugs, adult rats don't seem to like cannabis and it was not until experiments were done with adolescent rats that cannabis use was more acceptable to them. When comparing the consequences of THC administration, it was found that adolescent rats showed greater lasting memory deficits and brain changes than were seen in adult rats (Quinn et al. 2008).

In the 1970s, the first human studies were done that demonstrated profound tolerance after repeated administration (even when the experimental subjects and the researchers did not know whether THC or a placebo was being administered). The same study found withdrawal symptoms when THC was ceased abruptly (Ramesh et al. 2011).

Another way of exploring cannabis use disorders is to examine the extent to which the ICD or DSM symptoms are present in the community. A very high percentage (more than 85 per cent) of people classified as having cannabis dependence by both of these classification systems were identified as using cannabis to manage cannabis withdrawal symptoms, and failing to control their use or being able to abstain (Swift, Hall & Teesson 2001).

For the serious potologists, it should be noted that the endogenous cannabinoid system interacts with the endogenous opioid system, and tolerance to one affects the other. As previously mentioned, there is much more to the story of the mechanisms involved in the addictive properties of cannabis. These include the role of GABA and glutamate, acetylcholine, corticotrophin-releasing factor, sex hormones, oxytocin and adenosine (Maldonado et al. 2011). There is much more to be learnt, and hopefully it will lead to a medication that can assist in the management of cannabis withdrawal and the reduction of cravings.

What are the consequences of being dependent on cannabis?

People who are dependent on cannabis are at a higher risk of suffering from the negative consequences of using the drug, such as short-term memory impairment, mental health problems and respiratory diseases (if cannabis is smoked). Regular use and dependence can also lead to problems with finances, conflict in relationships with family and friends, and employment problems.

The risk of dependence increases markedly with frequency of use, with one in two daily users likely to become dependent. Rates of dependence tend to be higher among young people, who are more likely to develop cannabis dependence for a given dose than adults. This is especially the case when use is begun in early adolescence. It has been estimated that among young people who have used cannabis, one in six or seven will become dependent compared with one in ten of the overall population.

The weight of evidence from the laboratory to the treatment service for the existence of cannabis use disorders (dependence/addiction) is extremely solid and well accepted by all the scientific fields that contribute to the evidence base. The most controversial aspect of cannabis addiction is withdrawal. We frequently hear from regular users who do not believe that they experience any problems when they stop, and extrapolate from their experience to everyone else—no matter how their circumstances differ. The next chapter will explore this syndrome in more detail.

CHAPTER 6

You can quit: Cannabis withdrawal

Following are some of the comments we received on a story we had published about the use of a medication to help manage cannabis withdrawal (Allsop et al. 2014). While there were supportive posts, most were in this vein. The strength of the public conviction among cannabis users that cannabis is not addictive, and has no withdrawal symptoms when you stop abruptly, is amazing. It makes it very difficult for those who do have these experiences to talk about them with their cannabis-using friends, and to reach out to seek help.

> Cannabis withdrawal? Never heard that before, maybe cuz it's not true. I've been a pothead for ten years and recently had to stop a month ago for a new job and I feel pretty normal lol not one withdrawal yet. Keep my fingers crossed hahaha. (Chris Danger)

> Seriously...withdrawal symptoms???? This is apparently not science because marijuana has no physical

dependencies, therefore you can't experience withdrawal. Sensational BS, please take it down. (Thom Curry)

What?! I smoked marijuana for over 10 years and I quit cold turkey in 1 day! Any cravings is just out of boredom. This study is BS because there is no addiction to marijuana. It's all natural from Mother Earth! Man made pills are not natural and highly addictive! (True Chicano)

<Cited at Facebook.com/ScienceAlert, 19 January 2014>

While professionals in the addiction field have worked very hard to distance themselves from the notion that addiction is a manifestation of weak will—perhaps it has even gone too far in the opposite direction, with many now claiming addiction is a brain disease that means the addict is a completely helpless victim—these cannabis users often argue if anyone does report symptoms of withdrawal, then it is their weak will and nothing to do with the drug.

Cannabis withdrawal: Fact or fiction?

Even among those with no vested interest in the topic, it has long been believed that a major difference between cannabis and most other drugs is that no matter how heavily a person uses, they can stop using cannabis at any time without experiencing problems or symptoms of withdrawal. A similar view is that any withdrawal symptoms a person may think they are experiencing are actually not real, but purely in the person's head. Recently a cannabis user, 'John', who had quit cold turkey five days earlier, told us about feeling he might be going crazy. John couldn't understand why he'd been experiencing anxiety, mood swings, nightmares and attacks of shakes and sweats since he stopped using, since everyone knows cannabis is not an addictive substance. When he mentioned his symptoms to some of his cannabis-using friends, they told him that cannabis was not addictive, and either he had created these symptoms in his mind or they had always been a part of him, and the reason he used cannabis in the first place was so he could alleviate them. Another friend told him he was just 'mentally addicted', and that 'you clearly have an addictive personality and that is your problem, not marijuana'.

The advice John received from his 'friends' caused him a lot of needless concern, because his symptoms were in fact the result of cannabis withdrawal, which is now a firmly established reality. Since we now know that cannabis withdrawal is a genuine condition, it is important that regular users who want to quit are aware of the withdrawal effect that is experienced by many people during the quitting process. Knowing what to expect, as well as how to best deal with it, will be a great help in those first days of quitting cannabis. This chapter is dedicated to exploring the symptoms of cannabis withdrawal, the research supporting its existence and management strategies for people who wish to stop using cannabis.

What is cannabis withdrawal?

When people stop using cannabis after prolonged use (either because they cannot get any or because they are trying to quit), they may experience a variety of withdrawal symptoms. Below, we describe some of the most common symptoms that people have reported in the days after quitting cannabis. Bear in mind that not all people will experience these symptoms, and they do vary from person to person in strength, duration and the amount of distress they cause.

One of the most common cannabis withdrawal effects is sleep problems, which can include insomnia, strange dreams, restless sleep and night sweats. These symptoms usually start on the first night of quitting and can last as long as several weeks. As cannabis is often reported to be used to help people sleep, it is not surprising that sleep problems are a common consequence when the drug is taken away and the brain has to restore the natural cannabinoid system and readjust to those much lower endogenous cannabinoid levels.

The problems with sleep can also be made worse by the effects of other withdrawal symptoms such as headache, sweats and shakes, and stomach upsets. Many cannabis users who try to quit describe sleep problems as their primary reason for not succeeding at a quit attempt. One cannabis user who had made five attempts to quit described consistently losing his resolve on the third night of abstinence because the lack of sleep always overwhelmed him by that point. On the sixth attempt, he succeeded at quitting, and attributes this to the extra focus he put on tackling the sleep issue this time around. We'll talk more about dealing with sleep problems later in the chapter.

Another symptom that is very common among people in the first days of cannabis withdrawal is reduced appetite, often combined with nausea and perhaps vomiting. The nausea will most often occur before, during and after eating. People who have used cannabis to increase their appetite are especially likely to experience reductions in appetite and feelings of nausea when they quit. The consequences of reduced appetite are manifest in the average 1 kilogram (2.2 pound) weight loss typically experienced during a cannabis withdrawal. This is the opposite of the effect on appetite seen when quitting tobacco.

Predictably, cravings for cannabis are a regular occurrence when attempting to quit. These cravings tend to come and go, and can be stronger during times of stress, or in situations where a person would normally use cannabis. Although people who argue that there is no such thing as cannabis withdrawal would say that these cravings are purely psychological, in reality they are both psychological and physiological, as the brain readjusts to the lack of THC. This is supported by the very real physical symptoms in other body systems that are seen during cannabis withdrawal.

Another unsurprising fact is that a host of unpleasant psychological experiences can accompany cannabis withdrawal for the first few days, or sometimes longer. These can include mood swings, irritability, feelings of anger, trouble concentrating, depression, anxiety, restlessness and physical tension. Such experiences are due to the emotional response to the unpleasantness of the physical withdrawal symptoms, as well as the direct result on brain chemistry of withdrawing from cannabis. For example, receptors in the brain's cannabinoid system that provide relaxation and pleasure are no longer receiving the same level of stimulation that they previously were, and the brain takes a number of days or weeks to adjust to this change. Other documented symptoms of cannabis withdrawal include increased or decreased sex drive, diarrhoea, muscle twitches, boredom, increased appetite, chills, fever and stomach pain (Allsop et al. 2012).

Cannabis withdrawal symptoms can last up to a few weeks. While individual symptoms are often relatively mild, in combination they can strongly encourage continued use of cannabis and undermine efforts to quit. Withdrawal symptoms can be uncomfortable, but they are not dangerous. The symptoms are actually signals that the body is getting used to going without cannabis. So, while challenging to ride out, they can be seen as a good sign of progress towards no longer needing cannabis.

Evidence supporting the withdrawal effect

There have been a number of studies looking into the physical, psychological and behavioural effects of abruptly quitting cannabis after prolonged use. This body of research clearly points out patterns of symptoms that indicate a withdrawal effect similar to those produced by other drugs. While there are far too many studies for us to go over all of them, we have highlighted a few that illustrate the best evidence of the effects of cannabis withdrawal.

US researchers studied self-reported withdrawal symptoms in 104 frequent cannabis users who had made at least one previous attempt to quit. Eighty-nine per cent of the participants reported experiencing at least one cannabis withdrawal symptom, and 49 per cent reported experiencing four or more symptoms. To further support the existence of cannabis withdrawal, the symptoms fell into reliable psychological and physical clusters, and followed a consistent time course similar to that of withdrawal from other substances (Copersino et al. 2006).

In another study, researchers recruited 49 frequent cannabis users, and monitored their withdrawal symptoms daily during two weeks of abstinence. From this they developed and tested the soundness of a cannabis withdrawal scale, which measured the severity and duration of various withdrawal symptoms. Results found support for the reliability of the scale, and discovered that high scores on the scale were associated with higher levels of cannabis dependence, greater functional impairment and higher rates of relapse during the abstinence period (Allsop et al. 2012).

Researchers who reviewed existing animal and human studies examining cannabis withdrawal concluded that the evidence converged to indicate the existence of a cannabis withdrawal syndrome with predictable psychological, physical and behavioural symptoms, as well as a consistent time course. The authors further concluded that the severity and duration of the symptoms were not unlike those associated with withdrawal from other substances (Budney et al. 2004).

One of the 'gotcha' claims from sceptics of the existence of cannabis withdrawal is to argue that it is just tobacco withdrawal—even though most Americans and New Zealanders, for example, don't mix their cannabis with tobacco. A survey to compare the withdrawal discomfort that was experienced by 67 daily cannabis users and 54 daily tobacco users, all of whom had made a quit attempt in the previous 30 days, found no difference in the level of discomfort experienced by the two groups of abstainers, suggesting that the experience of cannabis withdrawal may be as powerful as that of nicotine withdrawal—and nicotine is the most addictive drug around (Budney et al. 2008). This study also reinforced the reports that cannabis withdrawal symptoms negatively affect the desire and ability to quit.

During the first few days of cannabis withdrawal, some people say mood swings and irritability become extreme enough to significantly affect their behaviour and their treatment of others around them. Studies of cannabis withdrawal have also examined this effect. One study did this by looking at aggressive game-play in heavy cannabis users during 28 days of abstinence (Kouri, Pope & Lukas 1999). The game, ostensibly aimed at measuring motor performance, was a computer push button game in which 100 presses of the A key would result in the participant receiving a point (and a payment of 50 cents for each point accumulated at the end of the game) and ten presses of the B key would result in an opponent who was simultaneously playing the game in another room losing a point. In reality, this opponent did not exist and the participant was actually playing only against the computer, which would take points from the participant on a set number of occasions. As there was no reward for beating the 'opponent' at the end of the challenge, pressing the B button could be considered an indicator of aggressive behaviour.

Participants played the game the day before abstaining from cannabis, then on days 1, 3, 7 and 28 of abstinence. Urine tests confirmed their abstinence throughout this period. The study found that the participants increased their aggressive play on days 3 and 7 of abstinence. Consistent with the time-limited withdrawal effect, their aggressive play had reduced down to pre-abstinence levels on day 28. The study included a comparison group of 20 non-cannabis users or infrequent users, who did not display changes in aggression throughout the study process.

A real-world parallel to this can be seen in one of our research participants, who told us about his withdrawal experience. Ken, a married 38-year-old man with two children, attempted to abstain from cannabis after using heavily for fifteen years. He said that the most intolerable withdrawal symptom he experienced was anger and irritability, which would at times lead to low-level aggression (e.g. becoming snappy or visibly annoyed with people when there was no justification for this). He also said that he was not as happy with his parenting because he had become less patient with his children and less tolerant of the day-to-day stresses that were an inevitable part of family life. After enduring two weeks of Ken's mood swings and aggressive behaviours, his wife—who had initially been a strong proponent of him quitting cannabis—handed him his bong. She told him he was unbearable when he was off cannabis and to go ahead and start using again. From there, he recommenced his daily use. This is one of the reasons why a small group of heavy, long-term cannabis users require admission to a treatment program to assist them withdraw where family are not supportive of home-based withdrawal because the behavioural consequences, such as very marked irritability through to anger and aggression, are simply unacceptable.

Another prominent, highly impairing and widely studied cannabis withdrawal symptom is sleep disturbance (Allsop et al., 2012). This withdrawal symptom has been examined objectively in a number of studies. Some studies have assessed sleep disturbance in cannabis abstinence using a gadget that monitors several body functions, including brain activity, eye movements, muscular activity and heart rhythm during sleep. One of these studies recorded measures on nights 1, 2, 7, 8 and 13 of quitting cannabis in heavy cannabis users. They found that, throughout the abstinence period, sleep was affected to the extent where sleep time, efficiency and amount of REM (rapid eye movement or dreaming) sleep decreased, whereas awake periods after sleep onset and periodic limb movements increased. Added to this, the more cannabis a person had used prior to the study, and the longer they had been smoking for, the worse their sleep disturbance was (Bolla et al. 2010).

In another study, this same gadget was used with heavy cannabis and/or alcohol users, and compared with matched non-users on nights 1-2 and 27-28 of abstinence from all drugs (Cohen-Zion et al. 2009). The study found that cannabis users experienced reduced slow-wave sleep compared with controls on night 2; however, by night 28, this was no longer the case. This is consistent with the existence of a time-limited cannabis withdrawal syndrome.

Nicotine withdrawal can also matter . . .
One thing that people who are trying to abstain from cannabis often don't consider is the possibility of experiencing nicotine withdrawal on top of cannabis withdrawal.

A degree of nicotine withdrawal is likely to be experienced by most cannabis users who use tobacco only to mix with cannabis, smoke cigarettes separately from cannabis or do both. The symptoms below are commonly associated with nicotine withdrawal. Recognising them can assist people in their attempt to quit cannabis because it enables them to pinpoint the reason why they are feeling the way they do, and to respond to the symptoms in the most effective way.

Like cannabis withdrawal, the symptoms of nicotine withdrawal are usually the worst during the first few days of quitting or reducing intake, and tend to last up to a few weeks (although, as with cannabis, certain experiences can bring on a craving long after this). Symptoms of nicotine withdrawal vary from person to person, and tend to be more intense in those who use more heavily. The symptoms of nicotine withdrawal commonly include irritability, anxiety, difficulty concentrating, restlessness, sleep problems, strong cravings for tobacco, increased appetite and headaches. Other symptoms that can occur are coughing as the lungs try to expel built-up tar and mucus, and tingling sensations and dizziness caused by increased oxygen in the blood.

Research into cannabis dependence has also looked at the effects of adding tobacco to cannabis. One study, for example, compared cannabis dependence symptoms among people who either combined cannabis with tobacco (by mixing the two or by smoking tobacco immediately after smoking cannabis) with people who used cannabis alone. The study found that the combined cannabis and tobacco users reported higher levels of cannabis dependence compared with those who used cannabis without any tobacco (Ream et al. 2008). This means that people who mix tobacco with cannabis may not only be worse off in that they experience both cannabis and tobacco withdrawal when attempting to quit, but they may also experience more severe cannabis withdrawal than people who use cannabis alone.

Struggling with cannabis (and nicotine) withdrawal

While cannabis withdrawal is only a temporary condition, for people who are trying hard not to use cannabis, it can pose a strong threat to their efforts during those first few days of abstinence. The problem can be compounded if the person is also experiencing nicotine withdrawal, making remaining abstinent from both cannabis and tobacco seem way too hard! Take the experience of Rhiannon, who sought help from us in giving up cannabis for good. Rhiannon wrote in a diary documenting her first week of attempting to quit cannabis cold turkey. Below are excerpts from each day, focusing on her experiences during the withdrawal process:

> *Day 1:* I'm so used to lighting up in the morning before I get going to kick-start the day and get me in the mood for doing things. Today for the first time in literally years, I didn't smoke pot in the morning. I went about my day-to-day activities sober, including doing a four-hour shift at the café, and I have to say it felt a little strange, especially having conversations with people who I usually only saw when I was quite stoned or at least a little relaxed from smoking weed earlier on. I wondered whether they noticed—to me it seemed so obvious that something

was different and that I was acting weird, but strangely no one even batted an eye. I guess things look different from the outside than how they seem on the inside. The four-hour shift went really slowly. I guess because I'm not used to working without pot and without looking forward to smoking more once I got home. It made it much more boring. But that's alright . . . I was prepared for that.

After my shift finished I realised I was exhausted. Also that my head was starting to throb and I felt a little shaky. I really felt like lighting up a joint at that point. But since I had sworn off pot, I decided it would be alright if I smoked a cigarette or two instead, even though I very rarely smoke tobacco other than when I use some in a joint. I wasn't too hungry, so just had some cheese and an apple for dinner, then headed straight to bed even though it was only 7.30pm.

Day 2: I think I only slept about two hours last night even though I felt so wiped out. And when I finally did sleep I had the freakiest dream. Woke up sweating hard and with the shakes and my sore head had become a migraine. This sucks! I was dying for a joint but lit up a cigarette instead. It is surprising to me because I only ever use tobacco to mix and I have never felt a craving for a cigarette before, but I guess actually I must be at least a bit nicotine dependent. I think this because the cigarette helped a little with the headache and the shakes. But I still felt really agitated and was so tempted to fix everything by smoking some weed. I have never felt the need to light up a joint so badly in my life. Called in sick to work . . . not a chance of making it in today. At this rate

I don't see how I'm going to hold out much longer without smoking a joint. It's my serious concern that I won't even keep my job if this continues! How do people actually see this through to the end when it feels so terrible?

Day 3: Today is my third day of going without weed, and I'm almost at breaking point. The anxiety and bad moods haven't stopped, I'm exhausted from another night of next to no sleep, and my stomach is so wobbly I can barely eat. I've managed not to smoke a cigarette though. I made the decision not to do that anymore because I know it's just another crutch and I need to feel that I'm really doing this right. Thank goodness I didn't have to work today! Dreading my nine-hour shift tomorrow. I really can't afford to call in sick for this one, so I'm going to have to find a way to do it. Hope the only answer isn't to light up . . . I really want make it this time around.

Day 4: Well, today was not as bad as I thought it would be! I was tired because I still only managed to get about five hours sleep last night, and still had some pretty crazy dreams. This isn't a lot of sleep, but it's actually quite an improvement on the last couple of days. The rest of my symptoms have also eased up a little. This is encouraging. I managed to eat a decent lunch and dinner, and didn't feel too shaky. On the down side I did find myself getting frustrated with people at work more easily than normal, and can't really explain to them it's because I'm quitting pot. But at the same time it kind of felt more normal interacting with people than it did the first day I worked without smoking a joint beforehand. It's like I'm getting used to the wall being taken down and it's really not that bad after all. I have to admit though that I did slip up a little and join everyone for a cigarette after closing time.

Day 5: Today I forced myself to get some vigorous, sweat-inducing exercise. It took a lot of effort to drag myself out the door, but when I did I went to the gym then jogged home. Even though I felt wrecked afterwards, I was surprised and actually quite impressed that I was still able to do this . . . it has been a while! My friend who I often smoke with came around this afternoon and pulled out the bong. When she offered me some I didn't feel so tempted—maybe something to do with just having exercised, I'm not sure. But all that running sure took it out of me. I was bored with my friend when she was stoned and I was straight so got her out the door! Bed early again and praying for a good night's sleep this time.

Day 6: I slept okay last night, but today I felt pretty low. I woke up with my head feeling heavy and in no mood to get up and get on with the day. I wonder whether this is part of the withdrawal process or if it's just the way I am when I don't smoke pot. Although I feel the world around me is becoming more normal, I'm not sure how I feel about it. Had a short shift at work today then took it easy. Ate well, had a long hot bath, then sat for a long time and read a book. Although it was all a bit of an effort, I did notice another good sign: I felt like I could focus on the book better and actually took in what I was reading. Before I would just read to drift off to sleep and barely take anything in. I'm not too sure what happened today with my moodiness, but hoping it's just temporary and I will feel a little more upbeat tomorrow.

Day 7: I haven't smoked a joint in a week now! I guess this might not sound like such a long time for someone who's never felt hooked on pot, but it's forever for someone who's smoked as much as I have the past couple of years. I'm still getting some insomnia and have felt some moodiness today. But I'm really seeing the light at the end of the tunnel now. I already feel sharper, my memory has noticeably improved, and I actually want to do things that interest me again—it's really made me become aware of how much time I would spend on the couch doing nothing before. It actually hadn't crossed my mind that there was anything wrong with that. Or that perhaps there were things I could be doing to make my life fuller and more interesting.

Today I noticed that I'm beginning to appreciate talking to people without being stoned too. It's actually strange to think how much I have relied on pot for most things, even including interacting with other people on an everyday basis. I'm really feeling my confidence in my ability to go without weed increasing. Don't get me wrong—I still know I've got a long way to go before I'm completely free from marijuana's pull, but I also know that it really can be done and I feel like the worst of it is finally over.

Rhiannon's experience represents a fairly typical cannabis withdrawal process, with the first few days being the worst in terms of physical and psychological withdrawal symptoms, and the symptoms gradually fading thereafter. Given that getting through the first days of withdrawal can be the greatest challenge in successfully quitting cannabis, it is important for quitters to do whatever they can to assist them in coping with this early stage of abstinence.

Another way to monitor your withdrawal is to use a questionnaire that we know is a sensitive measure of changes in the symptoms every morning. This is included in Chapter 9 (p. 160), but if you're interested in checking it out now, here is the link: <http://ncpic.org.au/static/pdfs/cannabis-withdrawal-scale.pdf>.

Coping with cannabis withdrawal
While methods of coping with cannabis withdrawal and other strategies to help with quitting cannabis will be addressed more fully in Chapter 9, below are the basic things to remember and do if you are experiencing cannabis withdrawal.

♦ First, expect to have strong cravings for cannabis. Urges to use cannabis are fairly inevitable when an everyday (or nearly everyday) user attempts to quit and is experiencing withdrawal. These urges tend to come and go in waves—they reach a 'peak' and then get weaker. It's like a wave rising up then passing you by. Knowing that they are short term will help a person handle them. This is called 'urge surfing'.

♦ When cravings feel strong, you can benefit from using a number of strategies. One is doing something unrelated to using cannabis, such as taking a walk, eating or calling a friend. Another is to delay use for as long as possible. To do this, check the time and make a deal with yourself not to use cannabis for at least half an hour. Do something else while you wait. After half an hour, decide whether you still really need to have a smoke. In most cases, the urge will largely have passed and the need will not seem anywhere near as strong.

- Keeping cravings in perspective is also important. For example, ask yourself how does it compare with a bad case of sunburn or being really stressed? Remember that a craving is uncomfortable but not unbearable; you don't have to be overwhelmed by it. Don't let it get out of proportion.

- Remembering the negatives of cannabis use can give that extra motivational kick that is needed during a craving. Often when having cravings, people tend to remember only the positive effects of smoking and forget the negatives. It can be useful to think of the negative effects of smoking and the benefits of not smoking.

- Another useful strategy is to avoid situations with strong personal triggers. For example, if you keep watching a movie with other people around you smoking cannabis, you will only be making these triggers stronger. If you tend to associate smoking cannabis with a certain place (for example, at a certain friend's house), being in that place is likely to bring on cravings and make withdrawal seem worse. If it is possible to avoid being in that place, it is best to do so—at least until you feel on top of the cravings.

- Cravings do go away, but they may be very strong for a while just after you quit or cut down. Remember that you win every time you beat a craving. It makes the craving weaker next time, and makes you more and more confident that you can resist a craving, no matter what the circumstances.

When experiencing withdrawal symptoms, it can be helpful to remember that they are positive signs. They actually show that the body is recovering and readapting to no longer being dependent on cannabis. They are short term, and it is impossible for them to persist for a great length of time—most will gradually resolve within seven to ten days. In the meantime, there are a number of things you can do to help manage the withdrawal symptoms and make the withdrawal process a little easier.

◆ Although this may be the last thing a person going through cannabis withdrawal feels like doing, many people say that exercise is extremely useful in alleviating withdrawal symptoms. First, it keeps you busy and occupied. Second, it helps to build confidence, self-esteem and a stronger attitude towards healthy living. Exercise can also help you to tire your body out, making it more likely that you will be able to fall asleep later on. The release of endorphins can counteract feelings of anxiety, depression, tension and irritability that often result from cannabis withdrawal. Another benefit of exercise is that it can assist the body to expel stored THC out of the fat cells. In addition to helping to get the THC out of your system faster, it also releases the THC into your bloodstream, which increases the levels in the brain, thereby perhaps reducing symptoms a little.

Some people also tell us that exercise has helped restore their appetite after cannabis withdrawal has left them with an upset stomach and not feeling hungry.

◆ Exercising earlier in the day is one thing that can help to promote sleep. But there are many other things you can also do to help. These include minimising your exposure to noise, light and any other disturbances; trying to go to bed at the same time every night (making sure this is a time you tend to feel sleepy); establishing a ritual before bedtime, such as having a (caffeine-free) hot drink and visiting the bathroom; and avoiding watching television, using smartphones or tablet devices or similar activities when in bed, as these tend to result in the bed being associated with wakefulness and the emitted light also stimulates the brain. If possible, resist the urge to sleep in or to nap during the day, and try to always get up at the same time, no matter how tired you feel. It will also be helpful to try to avoid caffeine altogether for the first few days of abstinence, to give yourself every possible advantage in getting good sleep. There is also reason to believe (although this is not yet well tested) that, like nicotine withdrawal, caffeine use at the same levels as when smoking is actually having a more powerful stimulant effect due to the interaction between the two drugs in the liver.

◆ Although you might not feel like eating much when first abstaining from cannabis, eating enough nutritious food can help you to feel better and to get past the withdrawal effects faster. If you are having difficulty eating, try to eat foods that are easier on the stomach, such as bananas, eggs, crackers, toast, oatmeal and green, leafy vegetables. Also drink plenty of water to assist with digestion and keep you hydrated.

There are many things you can do to help yourself deal with the emotional effects of cannabis withdrawal, including feelings of anxiety, depression, irritability and general stress. While exercising and looking after yourself will help, other activities aimed specifically to enhance your mood can also assist. Relaxation techniques such as deep-breathing exercises and meditation can help to relieve stress and anxiety. You can also boost your mood by planning regular activities that you enjoy. Be prepared for the mood swings and remind yourself that they are only temporary, and are a direct result of the withdrawal. If possible, plan the first week of quitting for a week that you anticipate to be relatively low stress. It can also help to seek some support and understanding from those around you, if this is possible.

A useful summary of strategies to manage cannabis withdrawal is the five Ds:

- *Distracting.* Try to think about something else, or do something that will take your mind off your symptoms.
- *Delaying.* If you have an urge to give in to the withdrawal symptoms by using cannabis, delay your decision to act on this. The feeling will usually pass in about fifteen minutes.
- *De-catastrophising* or not blowing things out of proportion. This means stopping yourself thinking that withdrawal is worse than it really is, and that the

only way to solve it is to give in to the craving. Remind yourself this is not the end of the world and that the symptoms will pass.

♦ *De-stressing.* This is about relaxation. Do something that will help you relax and counteract the withdrawal symptoms: go for a walk, have a warm bath, lie on the floor and listen to calm music.

♦ *Drinking plenty of water.* This will help with the detoxification process.

If you suspect you are also experiencing nicotine withdrawal, see your doctor and get a prescription for a low-dose nicotine replacement product for a short period of time (depending on where you live, this may reduce the cost) or buy it from a pharmacy/drugstore as it could be helpful. Be sure to do this only as a supplement to the strategies above, as these can also assist with nicotine withdrawal. Whatever you do, don't smoke (more) cigarettes!

Remember, if you are really struggling to get through the withdrawal symptoms on your own, seek some professional help. This could be from any number of sources, such as your family doctor, community health centre, a helpline or a reputable online quit program. More information about different sources of cannabis treatment is provided throughout this book.

In summary . . .

Contrary to the popular belief that cannabis is a benign, non-addictive drug that does not have a withdrawal syndrome associated with regular and/or heavy use, there is now a mass of anecdotal and scientific evidence showing that using cannabis can lead to both physiological and psychological dependence, and that stopping use is likely to lead to at least some symptoms of withdrawal, particularly if quitting is done abruptly. Anyone who uses cannabis or who is considering taking up its use should be aware that dependence is a risk. Those trying to quit cannabis will also benefit from being mindful of the dependence and withdrawal effects, and knowing how to best manage withdrawal in order to maximise their chances of quitting successfully. If these chapters on the harms associated with cannabis use have made you concerned about your own cannabis use or that of someone close to you, the remaining chapters cover tips for talking to someone about their cannabis use and provide a self-help guide to quitting (or at least cutting down).

CHAPTER 7

Changing behaviour: Tips for helping others

A feeling of helplessness and frustration emerges when someone you care for is doing something that you know or fear is doing them harm, and you can't get them to see things in the same way. As a result of our research projects and telephone services, we have been contacted by many parents, partners, employers, health and education professionals, and even children of regular cannabis smokers, concerned about how they can help others to recognise that they have a problem and assist them to quit—or at least get their use under control.

In this chapter, we examine the general topic of behaviour change and how it can be supported. In the next chapter, we will explore how to raise this sensitive topic and have more constructive conversations about any concerns that relate to a person's cannabis use and their options for change.

People use cannabis for many different reasons, and people also stop (or don't) for many different reasons. As we've already discussed, most people give up on their own, while some continue to struggle. While it may seem obvious why it is important for someone you know to consider stopping their cannabis use, for that person, accessing accurate information and getting treatment can often be difficult.

Annoyingly for the concerned friend or family member, motivation to make major changes in lifestyle can wax and wane as human behaviour change is a complex business. What works for one person may not work for another, what motivates one person towards change may not motivate another, and there are no absolutes or a perfect recipe. What *is* important is dogged persistence. Two other critical factors are timing and cost (and not just financial cost). Not only does the time need to be conducive to change, but the costs of maintaining the unwanted behaviour need to be considerable. Cannabis use does have its payoffs, which is why people do it, but smoking also has its drawbacks (pardon the pun) or costs. These include the negative health effects discussed earlier, financial burdens, relationship conflicts, problems with school and employment—the list goes on. Consequently, the point at which the costs of smoking become greater than the believed benefits is the time when smokers consider change. It is important to recognise that people have different levels of readiness to change a particular behaviour. Some may not think their behaviour needs changing—they don't see any problem with what they are doing. Some may have thought about it but not taken steps towards change, while others may have actively tried to change their behaviour in the past and relapsed. Fortunately, some have made multiple attempts at change and finally succeeded. Behaviour change is possible.

There are a number of schematic models of human behaviour change but a very well established one, known as the 'stages of change', was developed by Prochaska and DiClemente (1982). It provides a framework that explains the process of behaviour change. It evolved from the smoking cessation research, but it has also been used successfully to assist individuals in making a number of healthier lifestyle choices. In this model, successful change takes place when an individual is able to move through each of the stages of change. These stages are:

- *pre-contemplation*: when the individual is not considering change and they do not view their current behaviour as problematic
- *contemplation*: when the individual is starting to weigh up the pros and cons of their behaviour and is considering making a change
- *preparation*: when the individual becomes more committed to the idea of change, can see the benefits of change and starts to develop a change plan
- *action*: when the individual makes a specific change to their behaviour
- *maintenance*: when the individual works to maintain the change they have made until it becomes the norm.

The notion of relapse is also included in the theory. Relapse occurs when a person falls back into their old pattern of use and enters the cycle again. The 'stages of change' model proposes that during any attempt to change a behaviour, individuals may move forward and backwards between the stages multiple times. In turn, this model of behaviour change, has played a key role in the development of the 'motivational interviewing' technique (which will be discussed later within this chapter) in terms of viewing change as a series of gradual steps. The best approach to helping someone move into the next stage varies, especially between those who are pre-contemplators and those in action. When contemplating behaviour change, be aware of where in the change cycle you or the person you wish to speak with might be, as the strategy used needs to be appropriate to the 'stage of change', or mindset, a person is in.

The one feature that needs to be understood is that change—any change—is difficult, and often incurs resistance and reluctance from the person who needs to make these changes, especially if they feel judged or attacked for their past behaviour. This resistance and reluctance can be minimised by using the right words.

The most important tool we have to help others (and ourselves) is the words we use and the way we use them. They can inspire, crush, humiliate, motivate or make us ponder. It is therefore essential that we choose them carefully when talking to someone we care about, or for whom we are responsible, on such a delicate topic. The childhood saying 'sticks and stones may break my bones but words will never hurt me' is not entirely true. Words can be used as weapons or remedies. Some people use words to deliberately hurt others, to intimidate or bully, to ridicule or assert authority. Using words in this way rarely leads to positive outcomes. Therefore, the use of supportive or encouraging words will have a great chance of achieving the desired effect.

When talking to someone about such a delicate topic as their cannabis use, remember that a non-judgemental, non-confrontational and non-adversarial approach will have a better chance of achieving the desired result. This style of communication is known as motivational interviewing even though it is an approach rather than an interview.

The simple fact is that people can and do change. It all depends on how much and for what reason. Change is a very complex and difficult matter, where there is much to do, but it is worth it, and can be done if the person is ready, willing and able.

In summary

Change is often difficult, especially when a behaviour is integrated into every aspect of your life and involves doing many things in a very different way—from your daily routine of being stoned to making new friends, and engaging in new activities and hobbies. Be aware of this when preparing to talk to someone about their cannabis use, and think about their needs, goals and fears. When it comes to others, be supportive by recognising and responding to their needs. People do things for their reasons, not yours; people change for their own reasons, not yours; people change in their own time, not yours. Change is hard but certainly not impossible. There is an element of fear of the unknown and of something new. There is a need to bear in mind that fear is also a great motivator: it is when the fear of continuing the behaviour is greater than the fear of change that change has a chance to occur and be sustained. It should also be remembered that sustained change rarely happens in a single attempt, so expecting or demanding instant results is unrealistic. Try to resist the temptation of expecting unrealistic results, issuing deadlines or ultimatums, or offering glib solutions.

The next chapter offers some practical suggestions for how to have a meaningful discussion with someone about their cannabis use. These ideas have been shown to be effective for many people in a number of clinical studies of adolescent and adult cannabis smokers.

CHAPTER 8

Talking about cannabis use

This chapter is designed to give you some tips on how to talk to someone when you are concerned about their cannabis use. It is important to learn as much as you can about cannabis—a subject that has been covered in the first part of this book. It should be remembered, though, that a conversation about concerns can easily be derailed by only listing the possible harmful effects.

For those who are not in the position of being concerned about their child's cannabis use a few brief words on prevention. The main reason that a child doesn't use alcohol, tobacco or other drugs is because of their parents—because of their positive influence and the knowledge that it would disappoint them. That's why it is so important that parents build a strong relationship with their children and talk to them about those drugs—as soon as they are old enough to understand. It is just common sense, but here are some pointers.

- *Develop and maintain good communication with your child.* The better you know your children, the easier it will be to guide them towards positive activities and friendships. This can be achieved by talking to your children every day: share what happened to you and ask what happened to them during the day. Ask questions that kids can't answer with 'yes' or 'no', such as 'What was your favourite part of the day?' Ask your children for their opinions, and include them in making decisions. Show your children that you value their thoughts and input.

Be ready to talk to your children as early as the fourth grade, when they may first feel peer pressure to experiment with alcohol, drugs or cigarettes. It is important to listen to your child's concerns non-judgementally, and to reflect them back to the child to make it clear that you understand and don't want to preach.

♦ *Be involved in your child's life.* Young people are less likely to get involved with drugs when caring adults are a part of their lives. This just means the basic things like spending time doing something your child wants to do as often as possible (this doesn't necessarily mean anything expensive—just playing a game or reading a book). While it can be tough when working full time, it is important to support your child's activities by attending special events, like recitals and games, and praising them for their efforts. Help your child to manage problems by asking what is wrong when they seem upset and letting them know you are there to help is another one of those commonsense parenting tasks, even when we are busy or frazzled.

♦ *Make rules clear and enforce them consistently.* Research shows that when parents set harsh rules or no rules, kids are more likely to try drugs. The same principles that guided teaching self-control and safety when your child was a toddler will keep them safer as teenagers. This includes discussing what rules should be (when the child is old enough, as consultation enhances compliance) and the reasons for them, clear explanation of your expectations, and consequences in advance. If a rule is broken, be sure to enforce the consequences with parents/carers as a united voice. This teaches children to take responsibility for their actions. Be sure to give praise when your child follows rules and meets expectations, not just punishment when they are broken.

* *Be a positive role model.* Children imitate adults. It is important to demonstrate ways to solve problems, have fun and manage stress without using alcohol or drugs. It is also useful to point out examples of irresponsible behaviour, such as ones you see in movies or hear in music. Remember that *you* set the example. Avoid contradictions between your words and your actions. Use alcohol only in moderation, don't smoke cigarettes and never use drugs.

* *Help your children choose their friends wisely.* When children have friends who don't engage in risky behaviours, they are likely to resist them too. As well as helping your kids feel comfortable in social situations, get to know your children's friends and their families. In order to encourage positive relationships, involve your children in positive group activities, such as sports teams, scouting groups and after-school programs.

* *Talk to your children about drugs.* When parents talk to their children early and often about substance abuse,

kids are less likely to try drugs. Short discussions go a long way, so engage your children in a conversation. Ask what they know, how they feel and what they think about the issue. Talk to your children one on one and together, and educate yourself about alcohol, tobacco and other drug use before talking to your children. You will lose credibility if you don't have your facts right. Fortunately, you are now well armed with cannabis facts unless you've been skipping chapters! You might also want to set some time aside for you and your child to act out scenarios in which one person tries to pressure another to drink alcohol, smoke or use a drug, and figure out two or three ways to handle each situation and talk about which works best.

* *Remember that any time you spend together is the perfect time for a conversation, and have an ongoing conversation rather than giving a one-time speech.* The content of these conversations can include the effects of drugs on the body and the legal consequences of using drugs. Make it clear that you don't want your kids to use drugs and that you will be disappointed if they do; discuss the legal issues, including that a conviction for a drug offence can lead to time in prison in some countries, or cost someone a job, driver's licence or college loan.

Leading on to the next section, if your child has tried drugs, be honest about your disappointment, but emphasise that you still love them. The following story is typical.

A caller to our Cannabis Information and Helpline, who we'll call Robyn, is the mother of a 16-year-old son, Josh.

Last year Robyn found a bong in Josh's school bag and confronted him about it. She told Josh she didn't want him to use cannabis or any other drug. He told her to back off—he'd quit. Things appeared fine until the past few months. Robyn told us she was concerned, as her usually happy and outgoing son had become very moody, was spending a lot of time in his bedroom and was not playing sport, which is something he had always enjoyed in the past. On the weekend, she found a plastic bag containing what she suspected was cannabis. When she attempted to discuss it with her son, he got angry and defensive and told her cannabis was not harmful and she didn't know anything. Robyn said she was at her wit's end and was fearful for her son. She asked whether there was anything she could do.

The rest of this chapter is for those concerned about someone whose cannabis use is causing problems—if not for them at this point, then for those who love or work with them.

The time has come where a different conversation is required about someone's cannabis use. The previous chapters have armed you with the facts, but it is also important to be clear about what is known and relate that to how you see the person behaving. Some conversation starters with heavy cannabis smokers could commence with statements such as, 'I can tell this is hard to talk about, and I know I'm no expert about the effects of cannabis, but when I see you isolating yourself from your friends and giving up things that I know you used to love doing, I can't just sit and say nothing. I would do anything to see you happy again.' Or, 'When I see you're cranky and in a bad mood most of the time, I know something is going on and I worry about you. It concerns me to see you so unhappy. I am okay listening to anything you have to say and talking about this, as long as you know how much I love you and that I am always on your side.'

For those dealing with someone who is not yet using weekly or more often, an educated discussion of the short- and long-term harms of cannabis use is best—one that highlights any issues that you or the user have identified, along with any impact that smoking might be having in the present and future, as well as reinforcing that any use is risky and pointing to where that information can be found. There are two online assessments available: one for young people called Clear Your Vision (<http://clearyour vision.org.au>), which sets out the stories of four young people, discusses reduction and offers follow-up; and one for adults, Grassessment (<www.grassessment.org.au>), a website where cannabis use, problems and knowledge can be assessed without a commitment to making change from the outset.

It is daily users who are most at risk of developing problems, as discussed in the previous chapters. They will need several and more intensive discussions, which highlight the facts around how their current and future use is affecting specific areas, such as their health, social life or psychological wellbeing. In all cases, effective communication skills are the key. Before you embark on such a conversation, you may first need to check your own communication style: how you are feeling, your stress levels and motives. It is also advisable to check your motives prior to having this conversation. Is the aim of the conversation negotiating a solution, or is it aimed at exerting your own need for control over another person? Does it aim to resolve the situation, or just allow you to vent your own emotional state? You may be annoyed about how their behaviour is affecting your life; you may be afraid that the conversation might become awkward or emotional; or fearful that you may both become frustrated and angry if the discussion escalates into a heated argument as it becomes more personal and less factual. You may also be concerned that the person may not want to listen to your concerns or views, and may become even more alienated from you—which is the complete opposite of what you are trying to achieve.

These fears may be based on previous experiences when discussing sensitive subjects. Take your mind back to one or two of those conversations and think about what went wrong and what went right. This is a good starting point, as you don't want to repeat what did not work but will want to use what did work and build upon it.

The least effective ways of communicating your concerns are when you are angry, being alarmist, giving ultimatums, being confrontational and having unplanned discussions.

Before you start the conversation, check that your communication style is not one of the following:

- *ordering*—'Just do what I am telling you.' 'Use your willpower.'
- *advising*—'It's no big deal. All you need to do is say no.'
- *ridiculing*—'You are just weak.' 'Gosh you are hopeless.'
- *sympathising*—'You must feel terrible about yourself.'
- *threatening*—'If you don't stop, I will no longer be responsible for bailing you out.'

◆ *lecturing*–'Now look, I found out that smoking damages your lungs, reproductive system and your memory and attention–what more do you need to know?'

◆ *diagnosing*–'I know why you use–you've always been shy and need it to talk to people.' 'I know exactly what your problem is.'

◆ *undermining*–'I know you would fail anyway.'

◆ *moralising*–'Someone like you deserves better than to do this to themselves.'

◆ *judging*–'You really are a sheep doing what everyone else does.'

◆ *interrogating*–'Why are you doing this?'

The conversations most likely to succeed are the ones where you are better informed; where you listen more than you talk; and where you display empathy and stay calm. It is a good idea to have more than one conversation, where each person has a turn at putting their point of view across, leaving it for a few days or a week while the other formulates their views or counter-arguments.

Remember that these conversations need to occur in an atmosphere of goodwill, and be open, respectful and allow an interchange of ideas, views and knowledge. The conversation should not be used as a way to vent, punish, prove a point or control the situation or person. The characteristics required by the person trying to effect change are empathy, warmth, acceptance, good communication skills, confidence, respect, knowledge, encouragement, openness–in short, the ability to inspire reflection from the person to whom the user is speaking.

The following are some useful tips:

◆ *Gather information about cannabis and clarify what it is that worries you about cannabis use.* You already have the information from previous chapters, but you can update or go further in depth at a site such as <http://www.ncpic.org.au>, <www.drugabuse.gov/publications/drugfacts/marijuana> or <http://Learn-AboutMarijuanaWA.org>. Talk to as many people as you can to obtain varied views and attitudes about cannabis use. Using a variety of sources to obtain information suggests that you have not only taken the time to gather up-to-date information, but that you are also being open in your approach to learning about the drug and its effects. Collect current and accurate information on the street names of cannabis, how common its use is and the short and longer term consequences of smoking cannabis.

◆ *Set a mutually convenient time to talk.* Informing the person that there is something important that you want to discuss with them, and allocating a time for this, are important. Not only does it suggest that this is something that matters; it also allows the person to be ready for a sensitive subject rather than springing it on them when they are not expecting it, and so are even more defensive. The setting and timing of the message can influence the outcome of the conversation, so setting a convenient time and place should not be under-stated. For example, say: 'There's something important I'd really like to talk to you about. When can we make some time to talk?' or 'I'll let you decide on the time and you can get back to me a day before so I can reschedule anything I have on.' Getting a commitment might be tricky, but keep trying and be sure to give sound valid reasons for wanting to have this conversation. If the person remains non-committal, ask why this conversation is such a problem. Listen to the answer and say that you understand, but explain that this is important for both of you. Suggest other times and have the person think about it and get back to you with their decision. If they are still resistant to having this conversation, try again to get them to choose one of two or three times you offer. Remember, forcing them to agree to your timetable might be counterproductive, as no one likes to feel they are being pushed. Avoid having the person feel that they are not in control and that you have pushed them into a corner where the only option for them is to get defensive or push back. Try to be flexible so as to allow them to feel that they have some choice in the matter. Then request a confirmation of the agreed convenient time. You need to ensure that this is a private conversation that does not take place in front of others. There is a need to respect the person's privacy.

- *Express your feelings—set the tone.* If you are feeling a bit anxious or nervous, begin by admitting that the conversation is making you feel anxious, nervous, scared, worried ... express whatever you are feeling. Admitting how you feel and that this is a sensitive issue/topic can help diffuse the tension and may set a positive tone, making communication for both of you easier. For example, say: 'I guess there are some things that aren't easy to talk about. I want to talk about something that is important to me and I would like to get it right. I'm feeling very nervous. I know I'm not very good at this, but because this is important I am going to try and overcome my nervousness, I hope that you will give me the chance to talk about it and hear me out.'

♦ *Be genuine.* Confronting the problem can be very difficult when you are unsure how a person will react or what the outcome of the conversation will be; however, expressing your concerns has the potential to create a positive impact. When sensitive subjects are broached, some people become extremely defensive—particularly when you are talking about something in which they have a great investment—as talking about it feels threatening to them. They may try to put off the conversation by changing the subject. Don't be put off by this resistance or reluctance to talk, which is understandable, and continue—persevere. Perseverance and expressing empathy and your concern will usually be seen by the other person as a sign that you care. It is important for the other person to receive feedback on their behaviour, and how their behaviour affects them and the people around them. Be aware, however, that there are ways of doing this that are better than others, so be conscious of the words you choose, the tone of your voice and your body language. Try to listen attentively, give encouragement to speak, show appreciation, ask questions, be reassuring, make eye contact and return to your needs and concerns.

♦ *Take special notice of your tone of voice.* The person to whom you are speaking may very well know that their cannabis use meets with the disapproval of others, including those who they love and perhaps respect. Disapproval is often displayed in a person's tone of voice, facial expressions and body language, not just the words that are spoken. A helpful thought might be: 'Is this a tone I would like to hear if someone was raising a sensitive issue with me?' The tone needs to be neutral and inquiring. This means that emotions you may be feeling need to be kept in check throughout the conversation. Check for anger, disapproval, resentment, disappointment or contempt. Remember that your tone of voice reflects your respect, and your level of care and concern. For example, 'I've noticed you have been unmotivated to do anything lately and I'm concerned that things aren't going so well these days' or 'I've noticed that you seem to be pretty withdrawn from me lately and you are spending more time alone in your room—why is that?' or 'Please don't think that I am being critical. I'm just a little concerned—it's just that I have noticed you have been handing in your work later and later than the due dates and that you keep asking for extensions. Is everything OK? I know you guys have been smoking a lot lately. What impact might your cannabis use be having on these extensions?'

♦ *Express your concerns.* When expressing your concerns, it may be useful to talk about how you are feeling. This is helped by using 'I' statements—for example, 'When you do X, I feel Y. The next time you need to do X could you please think about Y?' Another way to do this is to practise breaking down what you are trying to say into three parts: the action you want to address, your response to this action and the preferred outcome:

Action: 'When you ask me for money (which is an objective description) out of the blue' not 'When you hassle me for money' (this is emotionally loaded).

Your response: 'I get worried' (describes the emotion in response to the action, which was asking for money) 'because it makes me think that you are using it to buy dope which is not what I want for you' (the action you desire) (there is no blame) rather than 'you're driving me insane with worry about your behaviour'.

Your preferred outcome: 'and what I would love is (no demand) for us to sit down and discuss money and your use of dope before this situation gets any worse.' Putting it all together the statement is as follows: 'When you ask me for money, I get worried because it makes me think that you are using it to buy dope which is not what I want for you. And what I would love is for us to sit down and discuss money and your use of dope before this situation gets any worse.'

This allows you to talk to the person in a way that does not blame them for how you feel. It simply allows you to express the facts and consequences, and shifts the onus from them to you.

The aim is to send a clear, clean (unpolluted) communication with the intention of minimising defensiveness. It's clear because it is brief and to the point. It's clean because it is unpolluted with blame, innuendos, shoulds, nevers and always. Another example is: 'When you use cannabis, it makes me worry about the risks you are taking and how it could affect your health or future goals. I just wanted to let you know how scared I am for you, I also wanted to let you know that I miss you and miss spending time with you' or 'I have been worried about your cannabis use this past year, particularly after what I have learnt. I'm concerned about the risks you may face in the future if you continue to use it. I just want to let you know how I am feeling. Would it be okay for us to sit down and have a talk about this? You can choose the time.' If you express your concerns in terms of how you are feeling, the cannabis user may be less likely to become defensive or refuse to talk about it.

- *Always look for the positive in the person to whom you are talking.* Remember that the person to whom you are talking has strengths and the potential to do great things. Let them know that their cannabis use is only one aspect of them as a person. Focusing on their strengths and good points will let them know you care, and provide a more balanced interaction. Look towards their achievements and their positive attributes. Find examples of things that you like about them and tell them. Avoid dwelling on the negatives—such as the result of using cannabis and the 'evils' of the drug and its use. Don't use the styles that block communication, as discussed earlier.

It is not a productive strategy to focus on why the person is using cannabis; instead, focus on what you see and what impact their smoking has on you. For example, say: 'You are so talented and have achieved so much. I know you're the expert on the reasons you use cannabis, and to be honest I'm not sure why you like smoking so much, but I am worried that it is going to hurt you or cause you problems in the long run and perhaps interfere with both your short- and long-term goals.'

- ◆ *Avoid debates on the topic.* Practise this conversation first on a close friend or relative. This will improve your confidence and allow the words to flow more easily. Don't be afraid to ask: 'Have you ever thought about cutting down or stopping your cannabis use?'; 'What are you thinking when you think about making a change?'; 'How do you feel about attempting this change?' A note if your cannabis user is in their teens: adolescence is a time of many changes, both emotionally and physically. During this time, young people pay more attention to their peers than to their family, community and the broader society. Ironically, this is an attempt to see themselves as individuals and to decide how they want their lives to be. It is a time of separation, individual identity and in extreme cases rebelliousness. Tread extra carefully, and remember when conversing with an adolescent to put yourself in their shoes. Keep your sentences short—and preferably only one sentence at a time—to avoid it turning into a lecture. Listen to them first and allow them to let off steam—they usually have plenty of it. Stay calm no matter how much they want to turn this into an argument that they can terminate by storming out in a rage. Be very careful not to paint yourself into a corner by handing out threats or ultimatums: these are traps for young players. Finally, pick your time and your fights: don't nag about trivial issues. Gather the big issues for discussion one at a time.

If all of the above fails, and the communication has broken down to the point where parents, family, friends, colleagues and the cannabis user can no longer listen to one another, then professional help may be the next step. As a relative, friend, or colleague, you can consult your doctor, a psychologist, a counsellor, or a drug and alcohol service in an effort to improve communication.

When someone is using cannabis regularly, it's likely that changing their use could be a challenge for them. Questions that may be going through the person's head could include: 'Will my friends still want to be my friends?'; 'Will my friends understand and be supportive of what I am doing?'; 'Will they understand why I want to cut down or stop, or will they criticise me?'; 'Will giving up the fun of using cannabis be worth it?'; 'How will I be able to cope without cannabis?'; 'What will I do when I feel bad?'; and 'How will I face a stressful situation without cannabis?' Offering simplistic solutions is rarely helpful, so avoid them and remember that both the recognition of the problem and the solution resides in the person to whom you are speaking, so ask them to generate answers. It helps to validate that change can be difficult and express that you understand their fears. For example, 'I'm sure this isn't going to be easy if you decide to make changes—I know how hard it was for me when I stopped smoking cigarettes. Change is hard but that's why everyone has to work hard at change.' Or, 'Perhaps you need to get more information and new skills to help you through. You might then need to put them into practice.' 'But if you decided you want to have a go at changing your cannabis use, I'd like you to know that you have my unconditional support, admiration and respect because it isn't that easy!'

In summary, don't do unto others as you would not have them do unto you. This is why it is important to practise what you preach and don't forget that you need to have or earn respect if you accept the role of guide and wish to be taken seriously. This may take some time. Finally, because we are all different, it is okay for others to have different views and experiences from our own, so point out people's strengths and understand their limitations.

The final chapter is a guide to reducing or quitting cannabis for those who are thinking about making a change. It includes a quick assessment for cannabis addiction and tools to help you assess cannabis-related problems, strengthen motivation to change, and monitor any withdrawal symptoms and improvements; there is also a self-monitoring sheet (on page 156). The previous chapters are useful to check back on at various points in this chapter. Good luck!

CHAPTER 9

Beating cannabis addiction

The first thing to remember is that most people quit using cannabis—even after many years—on their own. We have carried out research on how they do this, and not surprisingly it is by instinctively using the same techniques that we know work when used with a health professional. This chapter sets out lots of tools and techniques that you can pick up as you require them. It is not a strict recipe, but rather a menu from which to choose what works for you.

Let's start with a typical story that highlights some of the issues we discuss in this chapter. This is John's story: he called our helpline after seeing his family doctor. At the time, he was a 44-year-old male and had been smoking cannabis for 30 years. When he first called, he was smoking between 30 and 50 cones a day, which cost him an average of $150 a week. John was told by his GP that his lung health was being severely impacted by his current level of smoking. When he completed the SDS (explained on page 129) he was assessed as having a severe dependence on cannabis, scoring 13/15. Over the previous twelve months, John had not attempted to quit or reduce his use, although he knew his tolerance was increasing and his use was impacting many areas of his life. John reported that he mainly used cannabis to manage his mood, and because he was dependent. He reported that he thought it would be very difficult to stop smoking cannabis or go without it.

John was provided with information about cannabis dependence and withdrawal, and his reasons for wanting to quit were explored. John reported that his health and the impending birth of his first child were his most motivating reasons to give up. He was worried, as he'd felt really angry and anxious when he had gone without cannabis in the past. He was sick of wasting many hours lying around on the lounge in front of the TV pulling cones, and his partner was also sick of his behaviour. John agreed on a scheduled reduction and set a goal of smoking 30 cones a day maximum and limiting the number of cones per session to two. In the next week, John reported struggling with this reduction. It was suggested that, as he was regularly smoking inside the house, he move to smoking cannabis only outside so as to minimise the temptation of having it lying around.

He reported boredom, stress and hanging out with friends who smoked as his main triggers for using cannabis. John worked out that his perceived benefits of smoking were to help him relax and calm down and to socialise. He reported memory loss, reduced lung health, nausea, not being able to drive, depression and paranoia, and a major lack of motivation as the not so good things about his cannabis use. The enjoyable activities he could do to assist him to distract and delay his cannabis use included bike riding, de-cluttering his shed, walking and gardening. John again agreed to a further reduction in his use to 20 cones a day. Over the next week, John used strategies like keeping busy, cycling and gardening to avoid smoking. He also avoided friends who smoked. John had the support of his partner and a good friend who wasn't a cannabis user.

John followed the reduction schedule for a few days and then decided to quit altogether. When he last called the helpline six weeks later, he was abstinent and highly motivated to not smoke cannabis again. He was already noticing that he was breathing more easily. John was very excited about his future and the birth of his child, and felt like he had when he quit alcohol fifteen years earlier. He was now planning on a future without cannabis.

Are you dependent on cannabis?

Sometimes how we feel about our cannabis use is not the most reliable indicator of whether or not it is likely to be a problem. The following questionnaire is a quick way of assessing whether you are addicted to (dependent on) cannabis. It is called the Severity of Dependence Scale (SDS), and it assists in identifying whether or not someone is dependent and allows us to identify the extent. Try to be as honest as you can when circling the answer closest to the truth.

Self-talk

Before you embark on this challenging task, some preparation is needed. We discussed in the previous chapter

SEVERITY OF DEPENDENCE SCALE

Over the past three months:

1. Did you ever think your use of cannabis was out of control?
Never or almost never 0
Sometimes 1
Often 2
Always or nearly always 3

2. Did the prospect of missing a smoke make you very anxious or worried?
Never or almost never 0
Sometimes 1
Often 2
Always or nearly always 3

3. Did you worry about your use of cannabis?
Never or almost never 0
Sometimes 1
Often 2
Always or nearly always 3

4. Did you wish you could stop?
Never or almost never 0
Sometimes 1
Often 2
Always or nearly always 3

5. How difficult would you find it to stop or go without?
Never or almost never 0
Sometimes 1
Often 2
Always or nearly always 3

Now add up the answers ___/ 15

Please note there are two cut-off scores for dependence: one for adults (3) (Swift, Copeland & Hall 1998) and the other for people 19 years or under (4) (Martin et al. 2006). If a person scores more than the cut off for their age group, they are said to be dependent.
3–5—mild level of dependence
6–10—moderate level of dependence
11–15—severe level of dependence
<http://ncpic.org.au/static/pdfs/assessment-tools/severity-of-dependence-scale.pdf>

the importance of the words we use when speaking with others, but the words we silently use with ourselves are just as important. This is called 'self-talk' or internal dialogue, where our conscious thoughts are also composed of words. What we say to ourselves has an effect on how we feel, which in turn has a bearing on what we do—and ultimately who we become. But remember, not all thoughts have to translate into action; we have choices.

Watch your thoughts as they become words
Watch your words as they become your actions
Watch your actions as they become your habits
Watch your habits as they become your character
Watch your character as it becomes your destiny
What we think, we become.

—Margaret Thatcher

When you are trying to change something like very regular cannabis use, it is important to remember that it is a fundamental law of physics that energy equals output. This means that the more effort you put into changing your cannabis use, the greater the chances are of achieving the outcome you want for yourself and the people in your life. Most people who successfully quit have tried a few times and occasionally relapsed, so self-talk about lapses is important.

Sandy, like many other people, was really down on herself as she believed—incorrectly—that she had failed and was a hopeless case. After five years of trying to reduce her cannabis use, she found herself worse off than before. While still at university and after a pretty heavy smoking session, she found herself feeling panicked and having heart palpitations. After an hour of fear and breathlessness, she took herself to the doctor who told her it was just a panic attack and to take things easy. He also suggested she cut back on her cannabis use as this might be a contributing factor. Sandy was so shaken by this experience that she decided to obtain more information and quit smoking dope as she was terrified that this would happen again.

After a few weeks, Sandy had managed to quit using the skills she'd learnt and was doing quite well. Unfortunately, she let her vigilance slip and went out with smoking friends, and ended up joining them for a smoke. She told herself, 'Well, I will just smoke tonight and stop again tomorrow.' However, she continued to smoke the next morning and throughout the day, and by the end of that day felt a complete failure so began smoking daily and increased the amount she used even more. She had turned a lapse into a relapse.

Let's examine Sandy's beliefs and self-talk. She believes she is a failure because she gave in at the first opportunity. Second, she believes she will never change so she may as well not try again. As her cannabis use increased, her voluntary control got weaker. But is she really a failure? Why doesn't she believe she can change? Is this based on previous experience? Or could other factors be playing their part?

Let's look at some issues that may be related to relapse: it could be Sandy's lack of self-esteem that causes her to feel worthless, or her self-talk, or even her own personality or disposition to give in easily when faced with hard decisions. Let's examine these briefly in turn.

- *Self-esteem.* This is the respect we have for ourselves—
  the worth or value we place on our own wellbeing. The
  opinion we have of ourselves can come from external
  sources such as the praise of others, success or posses-
  sions, but primarily it comes from our own internal
  sources—that is, self-awareness and self-acceptance, and
  the ability to express ourselves constructively and know
  who we are. It is our job to build on our own self-esteem
  and not to rely on others or external sources to do it. It
  is the belief in oneself, regardless of what we have or
  haven't done, or have or haven't been told. We don't have
  to prove we are worthwhile. Our very existence makes
  us worthy of all that we wish for ourselves. Therefore,
  if you are trying to make positive changes, be kinder to
  yourself. Expose yourself to positive emotional energy.
  Day-to-day life depletes us of energy, hence the need to
  replace it from a positive source, so if self-esteem wasn't
  inserted from an early age, build it yourself.
- *Self-talk.* This is not about going mad because you are
  hearing voices. It actually is about giving yourself a good
  talking to. As discussed earlier, what we say to ourselves
  on a day-to-day basis is very much related to what we
  feel and do. We can play negative statements or positive
  statements in our heads. You know that loop—the one
  you've been playing all your life which is on repeat.
  Perhaps it was the one you recorded of your mother,
  father, sister, teacher or any other significant other. The
  point is that these are recorded messages placed there
  by other people in our early lives that continue until they
  are consciously examined. Hopefully those recordings
  were positive ones, making us feel worthwhile or clever

and that we could do anything if we tried—such as 'You can do this, it's not beyond you' or 'If other people can do this, so can I.' However, they could just as easily have been negative recordings about how hopeless we were or how we always did things wrong.

• *Disposition.* Finally, some of us have a disposition that is more robust and can more easily ignore such negative statements and let them slide off, while others are extremely sensitive to the words of others. When we are little, we sometimes believe them to be true as we haven't developed the ability to assess them critically and determine their veracity. We then continue to play these recordings without examining them as we grow older. And often life events conspire to suggest that these words are true. What we say to ourselves has a great impact on how we feel, which in turn impacts on how we behave. We are often unaware of our self-talk, but it has a powerful influence over our lives. It is often not what actually happens, or what others do, that upsets us; instead, it is how we interpret and talk to ourselves about it that creates the feeling, whether positive or negative.

Self-talk can be realistic or unrealistic, moderate or extreme. Remember that we choose the words so we can decide what we say to ourselves. The words we choose depend on some of our beliefs, which in turn become habitual—for example, 'I can't have fun without smoking.' This turns into the habit of smoking before you go out in the belief that it is necessary to have fun. And it is those habits that are hard to change. If you can talk to yourself rationally about how things really are, without distortion and with a greater insight, you will then be better able to accept and respond to new ways of thinking and behaving. On the other hand, if you talk to yourself irrationally about how things should or ought to be, how unfair everything is (in an emotional way), you will feel angry, unhappy or upset. This will make it harder to achieve your desired goal. It's the difference between 'I can never have fun without having a smoke' or 'I don't believe I did that, I can never do anything right' or 'I messed that up, but I have done it well before so let me try that again and see what happens', or 'I used to go out and have fun without a smoke, so it must be possible for me to have a good time without smoking.' One piece of self-talk that is common is about withdrawal. It goes along the lines of, 'This withdrawal is making me feel crap. I feel like I'm going to die' compared with 'Hey, what's the worst that can happen? No one has ever died from cannabis withdrawal.'

By changing your irrational, emotive self-talk to more rational, unemotional and tempered self-talk, you will feel more comfortable about what is happening and about your self-control, and you will be able to choose how you act or what to do. Self-talk is also about your expectations. They need to be realistic not only for you but for others too. What is needed is self-praise for trying, self-encouragement and a willingness to keep trying: 'If I try to cut down and don't do it, this means I am a failure' needs to be turned into 'Just because I tried and didn't succeed that time doesn't mean I'm a failure. In my life I have done many other things successfully. At least I tried and I can try again and see how it goes next time.' Be kinder to yourself. Give yourself a pat on the back for trying, for having a go. Give yourself permission to fall short of the mark. As long as you keep trying, that's the main thing. The clue to identifying negative self-talk is checking how you feel. Use thinking words rather than feeling words—for example, 'I think I will try something different next time' rather than 'I feel so disappointed in myself, I'm such an idiot'.

Now you've had feedback on your level of cannabis dependence and a guide to shaping up your self-talk, there are some more tough questions to ask yourself. Am I such a high-functioning cannabis user that I'm immune from experiencing problems in the future? Am I really that different from other cannabis users? Do I try and hide my cannabis use or dependence by living a double life? Am I scared about what would happen if I were to reduce or stop using? Do I really believe there will be no one there for me when I stop? What are my strengths and how can I use them to make changes? Who's in control here? You know this isn't going to be that easy, particularly since you've probably tried before. You may have felt like a failure because you have tried before and then reverted back to smoking. But change does happen and dogged persistence pays off. There is usually a trigger that dictates the timing of the decision to change, such as one debt too many, one argument too many, a child taken away, the loss of another job or even having to sell your iPad to buy dope.

Gather your support system

An important factor in a successful attempt at overcoming cannabis use is having access to an effective social support system—the most appropriate people from whom support can be obtained. These include family members or close friends who are understanding and sympathetic to your goals. Research suggests that social support significantly improves the outcome of a quit attempt. Think about the people who might undermine your attempt and the people who might help and support you in your efforts. Write their names down and think about the roles they might play. Perhaps their role may be to help you problem-solve or offer moral support; they could be someone who might help you share a workload or be there for you in an emergency. Another person's role could be as a distraction—someone who is fun and has a good sense of humour. Remember to ask them for what you need and be specific and direct. You can also lend support to others through a variety of volunteer work if you wish. This is a very worthwhile undertaking, as helping others is uplifting, resulting in positive feelings.

Quit or cut down?

You first must decide on your goal. Is it to cut down or stop? If it is to cut down, how much will it be: 10 per cent, 50 per cent, some smoke-free days? Which smoking occasions will it be: no smoking until evening or not smoking alone? If your goal is to quit altogether, will you go cold turkey or do it gradually? You need to decide what's best for you but, more importantly, what is realistically achievable. You need to consider the withdrawal process: it must not be so unpleasant that you give up when you experience a level of discomfort, nor should your reduction be so small that it results in no meaningful change.

Setting your goals

Begin by writing down what you want to achieve. It is best to be specific and measurable, so don't be afraid to commit to amounts or dates—such as cutting back from half an ounce (14 grams) a week to a quarter of an ounce (7 grams) a week, or cutting down from eight cones to four cones a day. You could use money as a measure—for example, 'My goal is only spending $80.00 per week instead of $150.00 per week' or 'My goal is to cut down my use to four cones a day which will cost $80.00 per week over the next two weeks, then I will cut it down again over the following two weeks.' Write these goals down and read them as often as you can.

Setting tasks and goals is the basis of controlling your cannabis use rather than cannabis controlling you. It is important to keep a few things in mind when setting goals and making plans you intend to stick to. You need to decide how you will achieve these goals—that is, which strategies you will use to achieve them. Once you have decided on a course of action, come up with some personal rules that will help you achieve these goals. If, for example, your goal is to cut down, you may apply the following strategy or rule: 'I won't smoke until I get home from work', or 'I won't smoke on Monday, Wednesday or Friday nights' or 'I won't buy any cannabis until I pay this electricity bill, so I will string out what I have until then.' Some stricter rules may need to be implemented in order to establish new behaviour patterns. Some examples might be: 'I will only smoke on Friday and Saturday nights between 8.00 p.m. and 10.00 p.m.' or 'I will only buy cannabis once a month and only buy 4 grams [0.3 ounce], which will have to last me the whole month.'

It is imperative to keep a record of how much, how often, when and where you smoke. You need to own the process of change, no matter how stressful or time-consuming it is. As John found, it is actually easier to quit rather than cut down, and even if your overall aim is to reduce rather than stop, there needs to be a substantial period of abstinence if you are to succeed in the long term.

Even though we know you are serious about changing your cannabis use, the following table may help bolster your determination even further.

Please complete the table by putting in the number that describes your pattern of use and deleting those that don't apply (e.g. ounces if you use grams).

Pattern of cannabis use

1. I typically buy _____ grams/ounces per week/fortnight/month/ or other that applies.

2. This typically costs $_____ per week and _____ (multiplied by 52) per year.

3. I typically smoke _____ cones/joints/vaporisers/edibles per day (write in the number and delete the preparations that don't apply).

4. On the days that I smoke cannabis, I am high/stoned for approximately ___ hours per day.

    Which is _____ hours per week and _____ hours (multiplied by four) per month.

5. If you mix your cannabis with tobacco or herbs, write the percentage of tobacco/herbs: approximately _____ (enter the % 0–100—that is, one part tobacco to two parts cannabis is 33%).

Now try to recall your use of cannabis in the past four weeks, and in the table below (see p. 141), write down how much you smoked, starting from yesterday and working backwards. Take special note of any significant events that may prompt your memory of you smoking more than usual—for example, pay day, an outing, a concert, a party, an argument or stressful event. This diary can also be found at: <http://ncpic.org.au/static/pdfs/assessment-tools/timeline-followback.pdf>.

When you have completed the calendar, each day should contain a response about whether you used cannabis and how much you used. Although we want you to complete the calendar as accurately as possible, we realise that it is hard to recall things perfectly. So if you're not exactly sure whether something happened on a Monday or a Thursday of a certain week, just give it your best guess. Or, if you can't remember whether you had two or four joints, choose the middle of the range. The important thing is that two to four joints is very different from six to eight joints.

Calculate and summarise the following:
I smoked ___ cones/joints over the past **year (x 12)**
I spent $___ on cannabis last **year**
I spent ___ hours per **year** stoned

If you are not yet convinced that you should cut down or quit, it would be helpful at this point to write down your reasons for attempting to quit or cut down (see table on p. 142). The reasons for change need to be very important to you. You will be able to see this by giving them a rating from 1-10 on how important these reasons are for you.

Cannabis monitoring over four weeks

Start date: (day/month/year) _____

Monday	Tuesday	Wednesday	Thursday	Friday	Saturday	Sunday
For example			Got paid and bought dope. Smoked two joints.	Stayed in and watched movie. Three joints.	James's birthday: two joints and four bongs.	One big joint to get to sleep.

Total past month _____ joints _____ cones

What are the reasons you want to cut down or quit?	
1. List your reasons	**Rate importance out of 10**
For example: I am sick of coughing my lungs up every morning when I get up, or *I've got to pay off my debts*	*8/10* *9/10*
List and rate your reasons below:	
2. Now think what the future costs of continuing to smoke are?	
For example: If I continue to smoke I will have to keep going to the doctor about this cough that hasn't improved, and possibly run the risk of further breathing problems like bronchitis, especially since I mull up with tobacco as well. It might even lead to some sort of cancer.	*10/10*
List and rate your reasons below:	
3. What are positive things about quitting or cutting down?	
For example: I would pay off my debts and perhaps would have more money, which I could then use to buy myself a new car.	*8/10*

List the positives below:

Now that you have documented your personal reasons for change in a tangible way, read the following list to see whether there are any other reasons for you to want this change, or things you dislike about smoking that you might have forgotten.

Please circle yes or no if, in the last three months:

You tended to smoke more on your own than you
used to.   Yes   No

You worry about meeting people you don't know
when stoned.   Yes   No

You spent more time with smoking friends than
other kinds of friends.   Yes   No

Some of your friends criticised you for smoking
too much.   Yes   No

You sold some of your belongings to buy cannabis.   Yes   No

You found yourself making excuses about money.   Yes   No

You were in trouble with the police due to your
smoking.   Yes   No

You were physically sick after smoking.   Yes   No

You had pains in your chest or lungs after a
smoking session.   Yes   No

You have been neglecting yourself physically.   Yes   No

You have felt depressed for more than a week.   Yes   No

You gave up recreational activities you once
enjoyed due to your smoking.   Yes   No

You found it hard to get the same enjoyment from
your usual interests.   Yes   No

Your general health has been poorer than usual.   Yes   No

You have been concerned about a lack of
motivation.   Yes   No

You worried about feelings of personal isolation or
  detachment.   Yes   No

You usually have a smoke in the morning, to get
  yourself going.   Yes   No

See Copeland et al. (2005); <http://ncpic.org.au/static/pdfs/assessment-tools/
cannabis-problems-questionnaire.pdf>.

Traps for young players—watch out for high-risk situations

We are creatures of habit, and learn through association, so your smoking is linked to external and internal
situations. Hence the next job is to identify those high-
risk situations (HRS) so that they can be better managed
or avoided altogether. These are situations that provide
the greatest temptation to smoke or result in difficulty
controlling use. External situations include people, places
or things—even the time of day. For example, if you usually
smoke with certain friends or you usually smoke at someone's house, you may have a strong desire to smoke when
you are with those people or in that situation. An example
of an internal situation might be one that evokes a feeling
such as having an argument or a fight with someone. It
could be being at work, where you are constantly stressed.
In turn, these may make you feel like a smoke, particularly
if it is a situation in which you typically smoke, often or
heavily, due to the feeling you get from that situation.

While some situations can be avoided, others cannot.
For example, if bedtime is a high-risk situation because
you need a smoke before going to bed, you can't avoid
bedtime and you certainly can't make yourself fall asleep
on demand; otherwise you wouldn't feel the need to smoke

at bedtime so you can go to sleep. Therefore, a new bedtime routine needs to be developed.

In order to increase your chances of long-term success and to prevent relapse, you will need to make plans for how you will deal with the HRS you are likely to encounter. It is important to start taking note of these situations—for example where you are, how you are feeling at the time and who you are with, as these may all be unique triggers. Triggers are specific feelings or events that prompt strong thoughts or cravings about wanting to have a smoke. There are internal triggers (certain moods or feeling) and external triggers (seeing a good deal of heads, having a few drinks, even payday). Perhaps in the past you may have found yourself in an uncomfortable situation and you smoked cannabis to help you get through it. Regardless, you now need to identify all these HRS and triggers to help you develop plans for better ways in which to cope with them.

What are your internal and external risky situations?

Remember that internal triggers relate to emotions and external ones relate to people, places or things that you associate with smoking. They could include getting home from work and walking in the door; feeling tired; needing to relax because you have had a day from hell; not having made plans for the weekend and feeling at a loss; or even a feeling of grief about missing your 'friend' cannabis.

In order to prepare and increase your chances of success, you should think carefully about your HRS. Here are some typical ones. Do they apply to you?

- a particular time of day when you typically have a smoke
- certain social situations, such as being at a party, or being with friends with whom you usually smoke
- particular mood states: these can be negative, such as feeling angry, sad or bored; or positive, such as feeling happy or celebrating
- being offered a joint or cone
- wanting to feel better, more relaxed or more confident
- having the thought that one cone or joint doesn't matter
- coming across cannabis unexpectedly.

To help you identify your main or most prominent high-risk situations, check your responses to the questions on the following pages.

So what have you learnt? What are the situations in which you are most confident that you would be able to resist using cannabis? What is it about those situations that makes you feel so confident? Is there something you can take from those situations to help you out with the situations in which you feel less confident?

Using the table on pages 148 and 149, identify all the situations for which you have scored less than 60 on a separate page, as these are your personal high-risk situations that require you to develop strategies to ensure they don't trip you up.

Before you complete the table, take time to choose four in each of the following categories and note whether any can be avoided or not, as avoiding the situation has the least amount of temptation associated with it. It's a bit like taking a job in a cake shop when you are trying to lose weight.

+ *Situations:* In what kind of situations are you more likely to use cannabis?

    1. _____
    2. _____
    3. _____
    4. _____

People: Who do you usually smoke with?

    1. _____
    2. _____
    3. _____
    4. _____

+ *Thoughts:* What kind of thoughts tend to lead you to use cannabis?

    1. _____
    2. _____
    3. _____
    4. _____

+ *Emotions:* What are some feelings that tend to lead you to use cannabis?

    1. _____
    2. _____
    3. _____
    4. _____

If you prepare for these situations, you will be very likely to resist the temptation to smoke cannabis when you are exposed to them. Failure to plan is one of the biggest reasons

Imagine yourself in each of the situations below. Place a circle on the scale to indicate how confident you are that you could stop yourself from (resist) smoking cannabis in each situation:

	Not at all confident	Somewhat unconfident	Slightly unconfident	Slightly confident	Somewhat confident	Very confident
If I was feeling angry	0	20	40	60	80	100
If I had trouble sleeping	0	20	40	60	80	100
If I remembered something good that happened	0	20	40	60	80	100
If I felt like I wanted to see if I could use again without becoming dependent	0	20	40	60	80	100
If I unexpectedly found some cannabis or saw something that strongly reminded me of smoking	0	20	40	60	80	100
If I felt I was treated unfairly or someone interfered with my plans	0	20	40	60	80	100

Imagine yourself in each of the situations below. Place a circle on the scale to indicate how confident you are that you could stop yourself from (resist) smoking cannabis in each situation:

	Not at all confident	Somewhat unconfident	Slightly unconfident	Slightly confident	Somewhat confident	Very confident
If I was out with friends and they kept suggesting we have a smoke	0	20	40	60	80	100
If I wanted to celebrate with a friend	0	20	40	60	80	100
If I was feeling sad about something or just for no reason	0	20	40	60	80	100
If I came home from work and just wanted to relax	0	20	40	60	80	100
If I was really worried about something	0	20	40	60	80	100

why people relapse. Most cannabis smoking happens without much apparent planning, effort or thought. Doing what you've always done is easy. So if you fail to plan, then plan to fail.

In order to succeed, you need to have a plan of attack. Avoiding your high-risk situations whenever possible is the easiest thing to do, and is extremely important in the first few weeks so you can build up your confidence. After you build up your confidence, you may be able to deal with more risky situations.

Some situations or people are always best avoided, such as your dealer. But even avoidance requires a plan. For example, what if your dealer lives next to your grocery store? If that's the case, you probably want to find a new grocery store. How will you get to this alternative store? What will you do if your dealer calls you? And what will you do if your dealer unexpectedly turns up somewhere?

Certain high-risk situations are unavoidable, such as different times of the day or moods. For these situations, you also need to plan ahead so that you will know what to do when they arise. If you typically smoke when bored, what will you do then? Life suddenly won't become more exciting on its own. You'll have to find a way to make it more exciting and/or learn how to deal with the boredom in another way. What would happen if you had a particularly nasty fight with someone? How would you calm yourself down? Who would you talk to? How would you make yourself feel better?

In the event that you may be a little short on ideas, here's some to think about:

◆ I will leave the situation or environment.
◆ I will delay the decision to smoke for 30 minutes

because I know that most cravings are time limited and I can wait it out.

♦   I will change my thoughts about smoking. I will remind myself that I don't need or want to smoke. I will remind myself about the negative consequences of having just one.

♦   I will go for a walk.

♦   I will remind myself of my successes to this point.

♦   I will distract myself by calling my list of emergency numbers or someone I enjoy talking to.

It's now time to go into rehearsal. Some people benefit from rehearsing drug-refusal skills. In short, these involve practising a simple, but confident statement to an imaginary smoking companion (one you can't avoid). Inform them that you have made a change and that you have given up smoking. Be clear and confident when making this statement. Be mindful of your body language when you are speaking. In a real situation, look the person offering you a smoke in the eye and clearly say 'No thanks'. Be careful not to say 'I am trying to give up' or 'I am trying to cut down'. The key to drug refusal is to state 'I don't smoke any more'. Spend a few minutes practising this, either with a friend or in the mirror. Try to sound as natural as possible while maintaining strict dedication to the task.

What are cravings?

It is time to discuss cravings and how to deal with them in a little more detail. Have you ever been really hungry and walked past a bakery, and been hit by that feeling in your stomach that went straight to your head when you thought, 'That smells so good! I am so hungry. I have to go in there and get something to eat.' That's a craving. Two things will make it easier to resist responding to cravings when trying to change your cannabis use. First, try not to get hungry: take care not to get into that situation. Second, if you *are* hungry, make sure that you are either nowhere near the bakery or at least are able to cross the road.

Virtually everyone who is dependent upon cannabis will experience cravings. These increase in intensity or frequency when you try to cut down or stop using cannabis. Essentially, cravings are urges to do the things you are trying to change—that is, use cannabis. While these feelings may be uncomfortable, it is possible to deal with them effectively. Understanding the nature of an urge is the first step towards becoming more successful at overcoming them. Cravings are generally not random; they usually occur in response to some event or situation that you associate with smoking cannabis. For example, it is almost guaranteed that your HRS will make you crave cannabis. This is because your brain has learned to associate HRS with using cannabis. You have used cannabis repeatedly in those situations. By doing so, your brain has learned that cannabis is coming. Some research has shown that your body starts to prepare for cannabis consumption in these situations. In other words, you might start to experience some withdrawal symptoms because your body is trying to compensate for what it believes is soon-to-be consumed cannabis. Hence you start to crave it!

It is important to know that cravings rarely last for more than 30 minutes at a time. Unfortunately, not everyone waits to find that out. The only way to combat urges is to not give in to them. Each time you smoke when you experience a craving, you end up giving more power to cravings. In other words, you increase the chance that cravings will occur again. The objective is to do the complete opposite.

There are two very good analogies in relation to cravings and behaviour. The first was referred to in Chapter 6, page 97; it is called 'urge surfing'. Urge surfing is a common technique to master urges to use. Think of the urges as ocean waves, which begin to swell and reach their peak intensity before subsiding and crashing to the shore. Consider the following: urges come and go in waves. Therefore, if they are feeling intense, try to distract yourself for a little while and you will soon notice that the worst has subsided. Imagine yourself riding a surfboard on a wave and that you have to really concentrate so that you don't fall off. Now ride that wave as it rises up to its peak level, and ride it all the way until it subsides before it crashes to the shore, leaving you feeling more comfortable and no longer desperate for a smoke. This is urge surfing. You will feel good about not giving in and allowing the craving wave to pass over you. You will feel a great sense of control when you don't fall off. Resisting smoking in the presence of an urge will help to weaken the urge over time until it finally disappears: you no longer have an urge to smoke, even in the most high-risk situation. Each time you overcome a bout of craving, it makes the cravings weaker for the next time, and it makes you stronger as your technique for resisting improves. The aim is to learn to surf and stay on that surfboard until you are in calm waters—in which case you will no longer need to surf and will remain in calm water from then on.

Another analogy involves cats. Urges can be compared with feeding a stray cat that continues to visit because you keep feeding it when it comes to the door crying. Think of cannabis urges as the cat crying loudly at the door. In the beginning, you may want to feed the cat because it cries for food and attention. You may find that it is a nice thing to do and you feel good about it. However harmless this seems, your act of feeding the cat encourages it to repeat its cries and attention seeking. You find yourself giving in each time because you need it to stop crying. Over a period of time, the cat grows bolder and starts scratching at the door, and perhaps other cats join in crying for food and your attention. You may begin to regret your actions, as a large number of strays are now scratching at the door and contributing to the noise, creating an even bigger problem. But you cannot ignore their cries. You may believe that their survival now depends on you, and that your actions are more important than ever. They have you trapped in a cycle of your own pattern of repeated problem behaviour. If you make a decision to resist feeding the 'cat army', there will be loud and pitiful cries for a few days or nights. In fact, they will be at their strongest when you have decided not to reinforce their behaviour. Soon, however, they will come to realise that you are no longer going to give them food and will gradually diminish in number and disappear. Your decision to stick with the action of not giving in and feeding them in order for them to stop crying is a win for you. It will 'undo' the problem that you unknowingly built up in the first place.

Urges *do* stop. They may be very strong for a short while immediately after quitting. However, knowing that urges weaken over time will help you resist the impulse to give in. So take back the control. Other methods for dealing with urges were discussed in Chapter 6, and will be reviewed again briefly here.

Strategies for change: Planning to quit or cut down

Now you have chosen the date and written down your personal plans, you will need to obtain a diary or a weekly planner and write down the date on which you intend to quit or change. Now look at the days after that change date and try to clear the decks as much as you can during that first week of quitting.

You will need to use another piece of paper to fill out what is called a self-monitor sheet. These sheets have been found to be very successful tools with people trying to quit smoking cigarettes as well as cannabis. Keeping tabs on your behaviour over time helps you slow down the automatic nature of a habitual behaviour. By using this strategy, you realise that a lot of cannabis use is not really enjoyed or needed, as many smokes are just automatically consumed without any conscious thought. On your monitor sheet, you need to keep a record of smoking and your cravings. You should record how strong the urge to smoke is (or was) on a scale of 1-10, along with the amount you smoked. You will also need to record the thoughts and feelings you were having at the time. There should also be a column for the outcome, which is also rated on a 1-10 scale. On the following page is an example of a monitor sheet that you can photocopy, or you can download a slightly different version at <http://ncpic.org.au/static/pdfs/daily-diary.pdf>.

High risk situations monitoring sheet

Date and time of craving	Situation	Strength or urge/ desire	Thoughts	Feeling	Outcome	Amount smoked	What I learned— score how I managed
20/5/14 Around 6.00 p.m.	Walked in the door at home.	7/10	There's no one home. I'm bored, why not have a smoke to kill time?	A bit lost, alone, sad, craving which happens every time I walk in the door at home.	Started mulling up. Why don't I like being alone? Why can't I just do something else?	3 cones	7/10 at least I thought about it twice and didn't just pick up the bong.
21/5/14 Around 6.00 p.m.	Walked in the door at home.	7/10	There's no one home. What can I do while I am waiting for company?	A bit lost, alone, sad, craving which happens every time I walk in the door at home.	I should do something else instead of mulling up. Maybe think about dinner to take my mind off it. Distracted myself for about 45 mins.	1 cone	5/10 by distracting myself for 45 mins I only smoked 1 cone.

Now you are ready to quit. However, nothing changes if you don't make it, so let's recap before we continue. You have:

- got up to date on the current scientific information in regards to cannabis
- learnt a little about human behaviour and behaviour change
- learnt about your level of cannabis dependence
- set some goals
- written down some personal rules
- recorded your reasons for change—that is, the downside of your smoking—while having identified what it is you want from this change
- learnt about cravings as well as having identified and written down your own HRS
- developed a self-monitoring sheet.

Now let's talk about withdrawal.

How to manage cannabis withdrawal

We discussed withdrawal in Chapter 6; however, it is worth briefly discussing it again. Severe withdrawal symptoms are the most significant factors preventing people from either trying to quit or continuing with their decision to change. They are one of the main reasons for relapsing. Many people are likely to experience at least some cannabis withdrawal symptoms, while some people may have little or no discomfort upon cessation. Usually, the psychological or subjective symptoms are most prominent. However, there may be some physical symptoms. These are uncomfortable but not dangerous. Perhaps you've experienced these before and you know how it works. And if you haven't, the following is a description of withdrawal symptoms.

The most common symptoms are sleeping difficulties, weird dreams and being irritable. Other symptoms are feeling anxious or nervous, as well as restless and on edge. The good thing is that all these withdrawal symptoms only last about seven to ten days (maybe two weeks at most). They generally peak in the first couple of days, so it is over and done with pretty quickly. After that, you will then start to feel a bit better. Remember Rhiannon? Go back to Chapter 6 and re-read her withdrawal diary.

It may not always feel like it, but withdrawal symptoms are actually signs that the body is recovering and readapting to being free of cannabis, so withdrawal symptoms are positive signs of recovery. As with the management of urges/cravings, the strategies of distracting, delaying, de-catastrophising (changing your self-talk from 'I can't do this' to 'it's not the end of the world . . . it will pass') and de-stressing (introducing relaxation) are recommended.

How well you cope with these symptoms will depend on your mind-set. We have already discussed that what you say to yourself impacts on how you feel. So you can choose to stop thinking about how bad you are feeling and start thinking about that footy game or yoga you love so much and want to get back to. You can monitor your withdrawal symptoms using the Cannabis Withdrawal Scale (Allsop et al. 2011), reproduced on page 160. Make as many copies as you need—some people like to fill it out morning and night to see how things have changed over the day.

Most of the uncomfortable withdrawal symptoms will come and go, just as urges to smoke come and go. Monitor your symptoms on a daily basis, as watching your symptoms reduce in number and intensity has been found to be extremely motivating because it results in a continuing endeavour towards the desired goal.

We have already discussed what to expect when you first quit, but be assured you won't feel all these symptoms at once. You need to consider that if you don't smoke tobacco but do mix your cannabis with it, you may also be experiencing some nicotine withdrawal. It is therefore important to calculate how much tobacco you mix into the cigarettes you smoke as you may want to use nicotine replacement therapy as well to assist in the management of withdrawal. Chapter 6 talks about the importance of not increasing your tobacco use when quitting cannabis. It has been found that it is actually easier to quit both cannabis and tobacco at the same time. This is because the high-risk situations for use of cannabis are usually the same as those for tobacco smoking. This is especially the case when the smoking rituals are very similar such as when preparing and smoking a hand-rolled cigarette to use the tobacco in a joint or cone.

The Seven Ds

The following is a fuller description of the five Ds discussed in Chapter 6, and for good measure we've added two extra Ds:

♦ *Delay*. When you first decide to quit, it can be hard. In the past, you haven't always been able to resist the temptation to use again. So on those really hard occasions,

Cannabis Withdrawal Scale

The following statements describe how you have felt over the past 24 hours. Circle the number that most closely represents your personal experience for each statement. For each statement, please rate its negative impact on normal daily activities on the same scale (0 = not at all to 10 = extremely), writing the number in the far right-hand column.

	Not at all			Moderately			Extremely				Negative impact on daily activities (0–10)
	0	1	2	3	4	5	6	7	8	9	10	
The only thing I could think about was smoking some cannabis												
I had a headache												
I had no appetite												
I felt nauseous (like vomiting)												
I felt nervous												
I had some angry outbursts												
I had mood swings												

I felt depressed											
I was easily irritated											
I imagined being stoned											
I felt restless											
I woke up early											
I had a stomach ache											
I had nightmares and/or strange dreams											
Life seemed like an uphill struggle											
I woke up sweating at night											
I had trouble getting to sleep at night											
I felt physically tense											
I had hot flushes											

This can be downloaded at <http://ncpic.org.au/static/pdfs/cannabis-withdrawal-scale.pdf>.

try telling yourself that you will delay using. At first, some people are only able to delay for ten minutes. But with practice you will be able to delay fifteen minutes, and then 20 minutes and so on. Sometimes it may seem like the cravings don't disappear after 30 minutes. But after keeping a daily diary, you will see that often you are actually experiencing new cravings triggered by a new event. Here is 20-year-old James's description:

When I first decided to quit, it was hard. I couldn't always resist the temptation. So on those really hard occasions, I delayed my use. At first I could only delay for six minutes. But once I did that a few times, I could then delay ten minutes, and then 20 minutes. Eventually, I could delay for 30 minutes and then eventually quit altogether.

◆ *Distract.* Distraction helps to delay and avoid using altogether. Depending on when you feel an urge, have different plans of attack. For example, if you have a craving in the morning, you can distract yourself by cooking some eggs and eating breakfast. If you have a craving in the afternoon, you can distract yourself by going for a walk or rearranging your work schedule. This was Sonya's experience:

Distraction helped me to delay and then to avoid use altogether. Depending on when I felt an urge, when I had a craving in the morning, I would distract myself by putting on a load of washing and hanging it out. If I had a craving in the afternoon, I would distract myself by going for a drive around to the shops. I learned the hard way that music was not a way to distract myself. It turned out that music was one of my high-risk situations. So in the beginning, every time I listened to music to distract myself, my cravings only got more intense!

◆ *De-catastrophise.* This means working on your self-talk. When you feel the urge to smoke, you feel like it's never going to go away and it can be hard not to immerse yourself in how powerful it feels. De-catastrophising refers to the tendency to become overwhelmed by the presence of an urge. When this occurs, there is a need to remind yourself that urges are not intolerable or unbearable, just temporarily uncomfortable. The following is Sam's experience:

Sometimes when I got the urge to smoke weed, I felt like it was never going to go away. It felt like the cravings would continue forever. It was hard to concentrate when I was feeling that way. One of the reasons I wanted to quit was because cannabis made it hard to think clearly. So if quitting was making my concentration worse, why would I want to quit? All this thinking was pretty quick and often I wasn't really in tune to all the details. But, by asking myself the question, 'Well, what is so bad about that?' over and over again helped me a lot. I did this until I finally figured out what I was so concerned about. Once I figured out I was concerned my concentration would never improve, I was able to de-catastrophise. I began to notice that I could actually concentrate at various points in the day. For example, I once played a game when I was experiencing a craving and ended up winning. That really showed me that I could concentrate, even when having a craving!

- *De-stress.* This is about relaxation, meditation and deep breathing. As previously suggested, doing exercise or going for a walk is not only distracting but de-stressing as well. You can also use a relaxation CD, choose an app or download some music. It might seem listening to a relaxation recording is pretty lame, but our clients find it really helpful. Play it every night before getting into bed as part of your new routine to help you find another way to fall asleep. It might not work every night, but it will help depending on your self-talk. Get a recording that teaches you progressive muscle relaxation and ways to relax.

- *Drink water.* Keeping up your fluid intake is important, as this is a physically stressful time as well, and you may be prone to sweating. This is especially important if you are increasing your daily activity, where replacing that fluid is important, and also helps the detoxification process.

- *Deal with it.* Own your decisions. Go back and look at your reasons for wanting to change and what you hope to achieve as a result of this change, then deal with the current discomfort. Take ownership and regain your control over the drug. Assess your level of readiness, willingness and ability. Use that self-talk to stop, slow down and become aware of what you are thinking rather than telling yourself how hard this is. Make the decision not to act upon the thought, and the chances are that the thought will soon pass.

- *Decide.* After a craving has passed, reflect on the level of your success. Every time you feel you have succeeded, you need to reward yourself, as this reinforces the new behaviour that you are working towards.

Plan a reward at the end of each day and week in which you are successful. Whenever you are giving up something you think is a reward, you need to replace it with something that actually is rewarding but doesn't have a downside. If you don't go out of your way to do this, you may start thinking negative thoughts such as 'What's the point? I'm not having any fun.' Perhaps you will become depressed, and this in turn may increase your cravings and thoughts of resuming your cannabis us. The new behaviour needs to be rewarding. Decide what is reasonable and appropriate for you. This is what Jodie had to say:

If I didn't constantly acknowledge my success, I often felt discouraged. Weed used to be a reward for me, so I had to find a healthier way to reward myself. When I didn't, I got bored and my cravings increased. I forgot how much I liked watching the blockbusters on the big screen with a big box of popcorn. I was scared that I would gain weight from doing this, but I decided eating popcorn once a week was healthier for me than smoking weed.

Take a few minutes now to come up with some ways that you can carry out the Ds.

How are you going to *delay*? _____
_____
_____

What will you do to *distract* yourself? _____
_____
_____

What can you say when you hear yourself catastrophising?

_____

_____

_____

How often will you *drink* water? How much water will you drink? How will you measure this? Will you take a bottle with you or buy water?

_____

_____

_____

How will you *de-stress?* _____

_____

_____

How will you deal with the thoughts swirling in your head?

_____

_____

_____

How have you decided to reward yourself? _____

_____

_____

How much money will you have saved? and what will you spend it on? _____

_____

_____

Who will you do these things with? _____

_____

_____

Putting it all together

Having looked at some of the issues that are related to your smoking, and having discussed strategies that can help you make this change successfully, there is a need to remember that change is a journey that has several stages. Like any journey, it requires preparation. The better you prepare, the more likely you are to reach your destination safely. As already pointed out, it requires dogged persistence and effort to be assured of success. It is important to remember that change does not occur in a straight line, and that the journey can be rewarding in parts and more difficult in others. Never lose sight of your destination. There is seldom one reliable map, and you will therefore have to chart the territory as you go. As you proceed, you will find that you are becoming more skilled at selecting the right strategy for each situation. You will also learn new strategies, depending on what your individual journey requires and how many times you have taken it. The key point here is to be prepared and plan ahead.

I'm not going to have to go through this again: Relapse prevention

We touched on lapsing and relapsing earlier, and defined a lapse as a 'slip-up'—smoking cannabis once you have decided to stop or smoking more frequently than you planned. A lapse does not necessarily lead to a relapse, which is returning to smoking cannabis in the same amount and pattern that you used before you decided to quit.

It is quite common for people to make mistakes when they are trying to learn any new task or skill. Becoming free of cannabis dependence is no different from learning any other skill. And just like any other skill, people do stumble occasionally. It is important to know that this does not mean failure, but is a temporary setback. Many people who are ultimately successful find that they have a slip-up along the way.

What is important for long-term success is how you handle that slip-up. Different ways of dealing with slip-ups depends on their type. One is lapsing on purpose, which can happen for a couple of reasons. Perhaps you think the change is becoming too much of an effort. You may get tired of working at your plan and decide to take a night off. Alternatively, you may decide that you deserve a reward for the hard work, and smoking is naturally your favourite way of rewarding yourself. These feelings certainly happen. If you find you have lapsed purposely for these reasons, you should think carefully about your reasons for wanting to quit in the first place. Focus on the original reasons for deciding to quit and think about how much these reasons still mean to you. Remind yourself that letting use go on for any length of time will lessen your chances of long-term success and make it harder to quickly get back on track as tolerance and dependence build again and cravings increase. You will inevitably kick yourself when you realise that the urge that led to the slip-up would have gone away in a short time anyway.

If you have had a slip-up because of exposure to a high-risk or tempting situation, despite your best intentions, you need to examine your overall quit strategies again. Ask yourself, 'What can be improved?'; 'Have I made a seemingly irrelevant decision along the way?'; 'Am I finding some high-risk situations too hard right now?'; 'How can I deal with them more effectively?' Doing some homework in this way will definitely help you to achieve these goals more effectively. Remember, the best thing is to get back on track as soon as possible, and remain positive about the overall effort you made, if you want to be successful in the long run.

After former smokers have been abstinent for a while, they often start to discover new aspects of life that weren't possible while smoking heavily. This is a reward in itself, on top of which you need to engage in activities that will be fun, make you feel better physically and give you more energy and enthusiasm for life. Keep in mind that things are what you make them, and you will find that the effort you are putting into quitting cannabis can later be channelled into developing other aspects of life that you would like to change or enhance.

Make a list of things that you would like to change or enhance, and note what effect smoking cannabis would have in attaining those goals. Of course, if you are adamant about stopping, you will see no role for cannabis in your new lifestyle, and a formal list of desired goals or aspirations will further reinforce that decision.

Many people find that the temptation to have a smoke may pop into their head every now and again, months and sometimes years after quitting. This is often a fleeting feeling, and is usually easy to deal with. Remind yourself that having such feelings does not mean that you have failed: it may be a natural response to certain potent triggers. Even after sustained quitting, you may sometimes feel a curiosity about what it would be like to have a cone or joint. One smoke will never undo several months of progress. However, having even one smoke—especially within six months of quitting—may greatly reduce your chances of long-term success. This is a very important issue, and a strategy for dealing with such a slip-up needs to be thought through. For example, you can consider whether the hard work that has been achieved is worth risking for the price of a minor urge to smoke.

It is time to consider the role of cannabis cessation within the whole of your lifestyle and how it fits with your personal aims and ambitions. Consider such simple issues as positive lifestyle and focus on health and wellbeing. You need to reflect on your efforts towards a balanced diet, exercise, personal fulfilment and recreational activities. Review the sort of non-drug activities that you are developing or currently enjoy, and reinforce the positive effect that such lifestyle changes will have in your future.

For those who are severely dependent and have been using every day for many years, quitting cannabis use is not easy—but nor is it impossible. Becoming free of cannabis dependence may be a reward in itself, but to many that is just the beginning. The opportunities that freedom from cannabis brings may include the reward of a lifestyle that users might have long dreamed about and certainly owe themselves.

You should develop an emergency plan in the event of a lapse. If you experience a lapse, you need to make a list of the strategies that you can employ. Here are a few examples:

- I will get rid of the cannabis.
- I will get away from the setting where I lapsed.
- I will remind myself that one smoke or even one day of smoking does not have to result in a full-blown relapse.

- I will not give in to feelings of guilt or blame myself because I know these feelings will pass in time.
- I will call for help from someone else.
- I will examine this lapse to learn from it by identifying the triggers and my reaction to them.
- I will explore what I expected cannabis to change or provide.
- I will set up a plan so that I will be able to cope with a similar situation in the future.

Remember that a lapse is only a temporary detour on the road to your desired destination.

Write down your emergency plan for coping with a relapse situation:

_____

_____

_____

_____

_____

_____

_____

Some people may benefit by obtaining additional help to address specific problems that have had a bearing on their cannabis use. There may be specific problems that need to be addressed: these may include further assistance with mood/affective disorders, counselling for early childhood experiences such as sexual or emotional abuse, or relationship counselling. Some people may benefit from a support group, and may appreciate being put in touch with others who have recently quit smoking cannabis.

Plan for success

As with any big task, being successful requires planning ahead and anticipation of trouble-spots. Virtually everybody who is successful says that it was not as bad as they thought it would be. It is the belief that it is going to be really difficult that puts people off and makes the job that much harder. Many people find that they need to clear the decks for a few days to minimise stress and other distracting hassles. Therefore, try to arrange to have someone to help or relieve some of your responsibilities for a short while. If you are employed, it would be good to take a week of leave to reduce the demands of everyday life and work hassles so you can take those walks or do other physical activities as you need to, in order to distract or de-stress.

Beware of rationalisations

At times, the going can be tough and it may seem that your mind plays tricks to get you to have a smoke. These are rationalisations: this is another term for making excuses to smoke — for example, 'I'm too busy to start today'; 'Just one last smoke'; 'It's a special occasion'; 'I've had a really hard day/week'; 'I'll do it tomorrow.' Awareness of these sorts of rationalisations will help you to deal with them better. Become aware that you are beginning to rationalise, and announce that fact to yourself in your self-talk. This is why we suggested earlier that it is a good idea to tell a friend you are quitting. Make a firm, positive statement to yourself, reinforcing your decision to change and your desire to be successful. This will help to short-circuit the strange twists that your mind can take when starting out.

Grief and loss

Smoking cannabis creeps up on you, and before you know it becomes a major part of your life. It starts to consume almost every thought: 'When am I going out to score?'; 'How much will I use?', 'How long will I be stoned for?'; or 'Will my work colleagues be able to tell?' And then, when you actually stop smoking and are successful in changing your habits and thinking about it, you become aware of a hole. Something is missing. It can feel like you have lost something very close to you—which in fact you have. Many people giving up tobacco, alcohol or drugs say they feel like they are losing a good friend—their best friend, in fact. It may be a bit like this for you. There might me a feeling of emptiness, of free time with nothing to fill it. For some people, stopping their cannabis use means spending less time with certain friends or feeling like they are missing out on stuff that they associated with smoking, like listening to music or watching movies or going to certain parties or rock concerts. Other cannabis smokers feel like they have lost their crutch—the thing that helped them cope with anything that happened. Such feelings do pass, although they take time. If you fill that free time with enjoyable activities, be assured that you will feel invigorated as you discover new possibilities and opportunities when your length of cannabis-free time increases—time that is spent engaging in either new adventures or re-engaging with activities that you once enjoyed.

Reviewing your progress

At the end of each successful week, you should reward yourself for a job well done. Often, people feel that they deserve a reward for all the hard work—and the best reward used to be, of course, a smoke. Be aware that this is a major pitfall. Have other rewards already worked out in advance, and be honest in acknowledging your achievements. Even if you have not been perfect, you should think of the good things that you have achieved and be proud of them. You need to turn yourself from a 'glass half-empty to a glass half-full' kind of person. If you have made mistakes or had problems, remain positive by examining what they were and learn from them.

Make a list of five or six reward options that will actually work for you:

_____

_____

_____

_____

_____

_____

At this point, it is important to think about strategies that have not been successful when trying to make changes in the past, and summarise them. Think of other strategies that you can use to help you to avoid making these same mistakes again next time. For example:

Problem: I thought I would test myself so I went to Jeff's place. Everyone was stoned. Before I realised it, I had a bong in my hand.

Remedies: A. avoid Jeff for a little longer; B. anticipate that you will again have to face the decision of whether to go and visit Jeff when you know that everyone goes to his place to smoke; C. if you must go to Jeff's again (and that conclusion really needs close examination), practise urge surfing and delaying use while at Jeff's place; and D. review coping plans in high-risk situations.

Self-monitoring
This can seem like a drag but it is really important so we're mentioning it again! Monitoring your urges and cravings, and your mastery of such situations, is one of the most effective ways to maintain focus and get the outcome you desire.

Planning
We have also pointed out that changing is hard work, requiring constant assessment of motivation, dogged persistence and lots of planning. Look to see whether there are any holes in your plan. This can be achieved by asking yourself some hard questions, such as, will my plan work:

- If I am tired?
- If I am having a bad day?
- If I'm having a really awesome day and want to celebrate?
- If I've gotten into an argument with someone?

- If my partner leaves me?
- If I get fired from my job?
- When I need to go for a job interview?
- If I'm feeling sick?
- If I find myself alone and thinking 'no one will ever know'?

We realise that some of these questions involve thinking about things most of us never want to think about. That's the ugly part of changing, but unfortunately when life gets us down we can be the most tempted to revert to our old behaviours. On the other hand, when something really great happens, we might also be tempted to do what we used to do: in this case, smoke cannabis. Old habits are hard to break, but not impossible. We need to unlearn things and learn do things differently. This is Dave's story:

Right after I quit smoking, I lost my job. The economy wasn't doing well, and my boss just couldn't afford to keep me on anymore. But it felt awful. I was angry. I'd put in six hard years for the company and this was how I got treated!!! I started to feel guilty and worthless and thought about how I'd shown up late to work maybe a few too many times. I also thought about how I got high on the job a few times. Maybe my off behaviour was what got me fired? But I had stopped. I was getting it together. So now, what was the point of remaining abstinent? Life sucked and seemed like it was never going to get better. At lease I had pot to fall back on. Cannabis, the friend who was always there—in the good times and in the bad. I had made plans that when feeling an urge to use I would go for a walk. But do you think I felt like going for a walk when I was unemployed and in debt? Err ... no! I started telling myself that walks were stupid. Walking is what people did when they didn't have a care in the world. I was in an opposite situation. All I wanted to do was sit on the couch and get stoned. I'm not going to lie ... I did just that. For two whole days, I did just that. And while cleaning up I came across a handout I had written, about not letting a lapse turn into a relapse. I remembered how in the beginning my motivation kept waxing and waning and that I didn't need to beat myself up if I didn't succeed at first. I figured that the most important thing after lapsing is not to fall back into my old habits and addictive lifestyle and rationalise everything. Not to mention being aware of the 'poor me' head spin.

I thought about why I had wanted to quit in the first place. It was to get a better job. I decided to call my mate who had been successful in quitting. We had a good chat and I realised that on top of all the planning, it is very important to have someone who can support you through the difficult times. It doesn't have to be a counsellor. It can be a friend, a family member, work mate, or someone from a support group or help line.

Coping plans should not be seen as rigid. You should do whatever works for you at that time. The coping plan you devise while working may not be the same coping plan that works while you are unemployed. Thus, if you are not successful in one situation, rework your plan. The point to all this is to find other ways to cope rather than using cannabis. So think about your situation. Try to think about the unexpected. How will your coping plan hold up? Are your coping plans vague or specific? You need to write out how you will enact each one. It is easy to say you will leave your mate's house when he starts getting out the weed, but it's quite another thing to actually leave. So how exactly will you do it? What exactly will you say?

Boost motivation

It is good to keep reminding yourself why you are making these changes—for example, to improve your health, get a partner, be able to travel. Motivation can come and go, so you may need a little boost during the times it becomes a little low. Think hard and increase the number of reasons for quitting by asking others to help you come up with more reasons. Ask anyone who is supportive of your endeavours. Give your reasons for change greater detail and more personal meaning. Try to imagine someone who doesn't use cannabis living out this benefit and write down things that show the benefits—for example, becoming a better partner or a more active parent. Write down the qualities of a good partner—for example, takes out the trash without being asked, does the dishes after dinner without being asked, comes home straight after work, calls when they are going to be late, pays attention while you are talking, displays affection, says nice positive things about their partner, smells good . . . you get the picture.

Here is another example: if you use cannabis to help you sleep you may consider a better alternative and write it down—for example, listen to relaxation tape, get electronic items out of the bedroom. This is better because it's not unhealthy like smoking cannabis: it's a better coping strategy, it won't stink like pot does, my partner will respect me for trying, I will eventually learn to fall asleep like other people do and I will feel so much better when I have control. And don't forget to reward yourself for trying!

Coping skills training

The more you attempt to avoid or deny problems or difficult situations, the more you will find yourself thinking about them, and in turn becoming more and more upset. The idea is not to avoid problems or unpleasant emotions, but rather develop better coping responses or coping styles—particularly those that make you feel better. Coping skills are an important part of maintaining the new behaviour change. Introducing better ways to look after yourself by having a more balanced and healthier diet, sleeping regularly and exercising will increase the chances of continuing along the path you have chosen.

Before we discuss helpful coping styles, let's define unhelpful coping styles, which can include:

♦ ignoring a problem or emotion by either pretending it's not happening or minimising it
♦ avoiding a problem by doing other things rather than dealing with a negative emotion or problem
♦ not being able to control your emotions by becoming aggressive, and yelling or swearing
♦ doing things on impulse rather than thinking things through first and weighing up the consequences of your actions.

Increasing activity levels—particularly of pleasant activities—helps to improve mood, acts as a distraction and helps restore a higher level of physical and mental functioning. When we feel bad, our emotions begin to spiral downwards (remember the impact of negative self-talk and catastrophising). For example, feeling unhappy leads to spending more time alone, which leads to being less active, which leads to feeling depressed and lonely, which leads to doing less, and so it spirals. The opposite is when we are enjoying or are successful at doing something, we feel good and our emotions lift so that we are more likely to do more of those things.

We recommend that you begin to write down one thing that makes you feel good every day. Write down the names of two people you can realistically spend time with whose company you enjoy, who make you laugh and share your sense of humour, then write down two activities you would like to do with them. Now record the names of two places where you have always wanted to spend more time, two things you would love to own that you can afford and two of your favourite foods. Write down seven ways in which you can relax and reduce stress (one for each day of the week). When thinking through this seven, choose a range of things that involve each of the five senses: sight, sound, touch, taste and smell. Here are some suggestions: running, reading a book, taking up or renewing a martial arts course, joining a gym, attending a stretch or yoga class, getting a shoulder, hands or feet massage. If you've been in a rut for a while, it might be useful to ask a non-smoking friend for ideas and contacts. Now write them down in your weekly planner.

Good sleep habits

If you've had a long-term problem getting to sleep due to smoking cannabis, you may feel anxious about falling to sleep without it. The following are some tips that you may find helpful:

- Introduce a regular sleep routine by going to bed at the same time every night and getting up as soon as you wake. This will help your body develop a regular sleep rhythm. Do not nap during the day. Follow the 30-minute rule. If you cannot fall asleep after 20–30 minutes, get up. Staying in bed when you are feeling restless and anxious is unlikely to result in sleep. Do something quiet and distracting like reading or having a warm bath. Try going back to bed, but if you still can't sleep, get up and do something. Do this as often as necessary until you fall asleep. Remember that bed is only for sleeping and sexual activity.
- If you wake up in the middle of the night, try to resist looking at the clock to see what time it is, as this may cause you to worry about not getting enough sleep. If you can't get back to sleep, get up and go into another room, and read a book or the newspaper until you feel sleepy again. Don't watch TV or read your emails, or even an iPad, as the light will stimulate the brain even without the content engaging you, and will help to keep your brain in the wake cycle.
- Do something physical during the day. Be active early in the morning or late in the afternoon, and go out into the sun. Avoid physical activity late in the day or at night.
- Make sure you are not too hot or cold. Turn off the television, phones and computers.

- Take up some form of relaxation. Do something relaxing 30 minutes before going to bed, such as meditation, taking a warm shower or bath, reading a book and drinking milk, or camomile or herbal tea.
- Avoid caffeine after lunch. Try to limit yourself to only having two coffees or caffeinated drinks a day.
- Avoid smoking cigarettes one to two hours before bed, as nicotine is a stimulant.
- *Important:* reduce your nicotine and alcohol intake during the first two to three weeks of quitting and above all do not substitute cannabis with another drug.

Plan to succeed

We have spent a lot of time on planning, because we have found a lack of planning is one of the main reasons for not successfully quitting. Your plans need to be detailed and reasonable. By putting together everything you've learnt about cannabis and how to make changes, you will be able to develop some pretty tight plans. You'll be able to avoid some of the pitfalls that many people have stumbled into.

We recently did a study that surveyed successful and unsuccessful cannabis quitters. We found that they engaged in eighteen different strategies that revolved around four components:

- stimulus removal (e.g. removing all smoking paraphernalia, adjusting routines to avoid HRS)
- motivation enhancement (e.g. writing up and rating reasons for change, consequences of not changing, benefits of change)

- distraction, and
- coping skills.

We found that unsuccessful quitters did not work on their motivation enhancement and did not develop coping strategies for withdrawal and relapse prevention. This indicates that unsuccessful quitters focus on the desire to quit, but do not sufficiently plan strategies for coping. Unsuccessful quitters also had significantly more symptoms of depression and stress, less education, lower exposure to formal treatment, higher day-to-day exposure to other cannabis users and higher cannabis dependence scores.

The findings suggest that working on coping skills and modifying your environment according to your various plans to manage withdrawal, craving and relapse are proven to enhance success in quitting cannabis (Rooke, Norberg & Copeland 2011). They also highlight that, while most people who are dependent on cannabis quit on their own, a significant proportion require some kind of professional assistance. If you have tried on your own using these strategies but don't have sufficient support because you have been isolated by your smoking for many years, or had particularly difficult withdrawal symptoms, then the next step is to speak to a health professional.

The other group of cannabis users more likely to need formal treatment are those who also suffer from mental health problems. Depression, anxiety, bipolar affective disorder or other psychoses—indeed, any condition where you might be using cannabis in an effort to cope but are actually in a vicious cycle, as Bob described in Chapter 5— can mean that professional treatment may be required.

Internet treatment

Cannabis smokers often don't feel comfortable in traditional drug treatment services, and sometimes drug treatment services aren't that willing to open their doors to them. As a result, an emerging means of delivering cannabis treatment is over the internet. Much of what is done during therapy sessions for cannabis reduction is amenable to online delivery. For example, a cognitive behavioural therapy program (as we've just described in this chapter) can largely be converted to a text or video web program, where you can complete the modules at your desired pace, interact with the program and receive automated feedback based on the information you enter.

Two such programs have been developed and evaluated in scientific trials. The first, *Quit the Shit* (Tossman et al. 2011), is a web-based cognitive behavioural therapy program that was tested for effectiveness when delivered in conjunction with online therapist support. The program was successful in assisting its users to reduce their cannabis use compared with cannabis users in a waitlist control group. The second program, *Reduce Your Use*, developed by NCPIC, is a web-based motivation enhancement/cognitive behavioural therapy program that was designed to be completely self-guided—that is, all treatment is delivered over the internet without a therapist. A recent scientific trial found that program users reduced their cannabis use significantly more than a control group who received access to a cannabis information-only website (Rooke et al. 2013). *Reduce Your Use* is available free of charge, and is completely anonymous and confidential. It can be found at <www.reduceyouruse.org.au>.

Being able to receive treatment for cannabis use over the internet rather than attending face-to-face therapy sessions can assist in overcoming many of the barriers to seeking treatment. These can include things like time restrictions, access difficulties, transportation problems, difficulty finding child care, concerns about the stigma associated with being in 'drug treatment' and privacy. Thus, for some people, getting treatment for cannabis dependence online is ideal. For others, such as those with co-occurring mental health problems, this form of treatment might not be suitable, or should only be used as an adjunct to other treatment, rather than being the sole form of treatment provided.

Other treatment options

Another free (in Australia) and anonymous option that has been shown to be effective in a scientific trial is cognitive behavioural treatment delivered via the telephone. There is a free Australian national number, 1800 304050, where treatment can be offered over about four sessions (more or less as required). This is a great place to start if you don't feel ready to try formal treatment. Work out the time difference and check <http://ncpic.org.au/ncpic/helpline> for the business hours.

Another place to start might be to have a chat with your family doctor, school or university counsellor or a psychologist. For a range of treatment options, see <http://ncpic.org.au/ncpic/links/treatment> for links to a wide variety of treatments from community counselling, detoxification services and rehabilitation programs. For readers in other countries, check with your local or national drug and alcohol advisory services or health departments.

Last word

If you put everything you've learnt reading this book into action, you will be on the road to success. If you have the desire to change, and you work hard at maintaining your coping plans, and revising them as necessary, you will succeed. Your cravings to use cannabis will decrease with each day of success. Trust us, cannabis will not be the first thing you think about when waking up in the morning for the rest of your life!

References

Aggarwal S.K. 2013, 'Cannabinergic pain medicine: A concise clinical primer and survey of randomized-controlled trial results', *The Clinical Journal of Pain*, vol. 29, no. 2, pp. 162–71.

Agrawal A. et al. 2004, 'A twin study of early cannabis use and subsequent use and abuse/dependence of other illicit drugs', *Psychological Medicine*, vol. 34, pp. 1227–37.

Aldington, S. et al. 2007, 'Effects of cannabis on pulmonary structure, function and symptoms', *Thorax*, vol. 62, pp. 1058–63.

Allsop, D., Copeland, J., Norberg, M., Fu, S., Molar, A., Lewis, J. & Budney, A. 2012, 'Quantifying the clinical significance of cannabis withdrawal', *PLoS ONE* 7(9): e44864.

Allsop, D., Copeland, J., Lintzeris, N. et al. 2014, 'Cannabinoid replacement therapy for management of cannabis withdrawal: a randomized controlled trial of Nabiximols', *JAMA Psychiatry online* doi:10.1001/jamapsychiatry.2013.3947.

Allsop, D, Norberg, M., Copeland, J., Fu, S. & Budney, A.J. 2011, 'The Cannabis Withdrawal Scale development: Patterns and predictors of cannabis withdrawal and distress', *Drug and Alcohol Dependence*, vol. 119, pp. 123–9.

American Psychiatric Association (APA) 2013, *Diagnostic and Statistical Manual of Mental Disorders*, 5th edn, American Psychiatric Publishing, Arlington, VA.

Anthony J. 2006, 'The epidemiology of cannabis dependence', in R.A. Roffman & R.S. Stephens (eds), *Cannabis Dependence: Its Nature, Consequences and Treatment*, Cambridge University Press, Cambridge, pp. 58–105.

Ashbridge, M., Hayden, J.A. & Cartwright J.L. 2012, 'Acute cannabis consumption and motor vehicle collision risk: Systematic review of observational studies and meta analysis', *British Medical Journal*, vol. 9, no. 344, p. e536.

Atakan, Z. 2012, 'Cannabis, a complex plant: Different compounds and different effects on individuals', *Therapeutic Advances in Psychopharmacology*, vol. 2, no. 6, pp. 241-54.

Australian Institute of Health and Welfare (AIHW) 2011, *2010 National Drug Strategy Household Survey Report, Drug Statistics Survey No. 25*, cat. no. PHE 145, AIHW, Canberra.

Banbury, A., Zask, A., Carter, S., Van Beurden, E. & Copeland, J. 2013, 'Smoking mull: A grounded theory model on the dynamics of combined tobacco and cannabis use among men', *Health Promotion Journal of Australia*, vol. 24, no. 2, pp. 143-50.

Bolla, K.I., Lesage, S.R., Gamalso, C.E., Neubauer, D.N., Wang, N.Y., Funderburk, F.R., Allen, R.P., David, P.M. & Cadet, J.L. 2010, 'Polysomnogram changes in marijuana users who report sleep disturbance during prior abstinence', *Sleep Medicine*, vol. 11, no. 9, pp. 882-9.

Borgelt, L.M. et al. 2013, 'The pharmacologic and clinical effects of medical cannabis', *Pharmacotherapy*, vol. 33, pp. 195-209.

Budney A.J., Hughes, J.R., Moore, B.A. & Vandrey, R. 2004, 'Review of the validity and significance of cannabis withdrawal syndrome', *American Journal of Psychiatry*, vol. 161, no. 11, pp. 1967-77.

Budney, A.J., Vandrey, R.G., Hughes, J.R., Thostenson, J.D. & Bursac, Z. 2008, 'Comparison of cannabis and tobacco withdrawal: severity and contribution to relapse', *Journal of Substance Abuse Treatment*, vol. 35, pp. 362-8.

Burns, J.K. 2013, 'Pathways from cannabis use to psychosis: A review of the evidence', *Frontiers in Psychiatry*, vol. 3, no. 128, pp. 1-2.

Cadet, J.L., Bisago, V. & Milroy C.M. 2014, 'Neuropathology of substance use disorders', *Acta Neuropathology*, vol. 127, pp. 91-107.

Clausen,L., Hjorthoj, CR., Thorup, A., Jeppesen, P., Petersen, L., Bertelsen, M. & Nordentoft, M. 2014, 'Change in cannabis use, clinical symptoms and social functioning among patients with first-episode psychosis: a 5-year follow-up study of patients in the OPUS trial', *Psychological Medicine*, vol. 44, no. 1, pp. 117-26.

Cohen-Zion, M., Drummon, S.P. Padula, C.B., Winward, J., Kanady, J., Medina, K.L. & Tapert, S.F. 2009, 'Sleep architecture in adolescent marijuana and alcohol users during acute and extended abstinence', *Addictive Behaviors*, vol. 34, no. 11, pp. 976-9.

Copeland, J., Gerber, S. & Swift, W. 2006, *Evidence-based Answers to Cannabis Questions: A Review of the Literature*, report to the Australian National Council on Drugs, Canberra.

Copeland, J., Gilmore, S., Gates, P. & Swift W. 2005, 'The Cannabis Problems Questionnaire: Factor, structure, reliability and validity', *Drug and Alcohol Dependence*, vol. 80, pp. 313-19.

Copersino, M.L., Boyd, S.J., Tashkin, D.P., Huetsis, M.A., Heishman, S.J., Fermand, J.C., Simmons, M.S. and Gorelick, D.A. 2006, 'Cannabis withdrawal among non-treatment-seeking adult cannabis users', *American Journal of Addiction*, vol. 15, pp. 8-14.

Crippa, J.A., Zuardi, A.W., Martín-Santos, Bhattacharyya, S., Atakan, Z., McGuire, P. & Fusar-Poli, P. 2009, 'Cannabis and anxiety: A critical review of the evidence', *Human Psychopharmacology: Clinical and Experimental*, vol. 24, no. 7, pp. 515-23.

Danovitch, L. & Gorelik, D.A. 2012, 'State of the art treatments for cannabis dependence', *Psychiatric Clinics of North America*, vol. 35 no. 2, pp. 309-26.

Degenhardt, L. et al. 2010, 'Evaluating the drug use "gateway" theory using cross-national data: Consistency and associations of the order of initiation of drug use among participants in the WHO World Mental Health Surveys', *Drug and Alcohol Dependence*, vol. 108, pp. 84-97.

Deiana, S. 2012, 'Medical use of cannabis. Cannabidiol—a new light for schizophrenia', *Drug Testing and Analysis*, vol. 5, pp. 46-51.

Ellgren, M., Spano, S.M. & Hurd, Y.L. 2007, 'Adolescent cannabis exposure alters opiate intake and opioid limbic neuronal populations in adult rats', *Neuropsychopharmacology*, vol. 3, pp. 607-15.

EMCDDA 2008, *A Cannabis Reader: Global Issues and Local Experiences*, European Monitoring Centre for Drugs and Drug Addiction, Lisbon.

Feldman, M.L. & Hadfield, S. 2009, 'Pot paresis: Marijuana and a case of hypokalemic periodic paralysis', *Journal of Emergency Medicine*, vol. 36, no. 3, pp. 236-8.

Fitzgerald, K., Bronstein, A.C. & Newquist, K. 2013, 'Marijuana poisoning', *Topics in Companion Animal Medicine*, vol. 28, pp. 8-12.

Ford, D.E., Vu, H.T. & Anthony J.C. 2002, 'Marijuana use and cessation of tobacco smoking in adults from a community sample', *Drug and Alcohol Dependence,* vol. 67, pp. 243-8.

Fraser G.A. 2009, 'The use of a synthetic cannabinoid in the management of treatment-resistant nightmares in Post Traumatic Stress Disorder (PTSD)', *CNS Neuroscience & Therapeutics*, vol. 15, pp. 84-8.

Gates, P.J., Albertella, L. & Copeland J. 2014 in press, 'Effects of cannabis administration on sleep: A review of the literature', http://dx.doi.org/10.1016/j.smrv.2014.02.005.

Gfroerer, J.C., Wu, L.-T. & Penne, M.A. 2002, *Initiation of Marijuana Use: Trends, Patterns, and Implications*, Substance Abuse and Mental Health Services Administration, Rockville, MD.

Gieringer, D. 2000, 'Marijuana water pipe and vaporizer study', *Multidisciplinary Association for Psychedelic Studies*, vol. 6, <www.maps.org/news-letters/v06n3/06359mj1.html>.

Hartman, R.L. & Huestis, M.A. 2013, 'Cannabis effects on driving', *Clinical Chemistry*, vol. 59, no. 3, pp. 478-92.

Hartung, B. et al. 2014 in press, 'Sudden unexpected death under acute influence of cannabis', *Forensic Science International*, http://dx.doi.org/10.1016/j.forsciint.2014.02.001.

Heinz, A., Deserno, L. & Reininghaus, U. 2013, 'Urbanicity, social adversity and psychosis', *World Psychiatry*, vol. 12, pp. 187-97.

Isaac, M., Isaac, M. & Holloway, F. 2005, 'Is cannabis an anti-psychotic? The experience of psychiatric intensive care', *Human Psychopharmacology and Clinical Experience*, vol. 20, pp. 207-10.

Kouri, E.M., Pope, H.G. Jr. & Lukas, S.E. 1999, 'Changes in aggressive behaviour during withdrawal from long-term marijuana use', *Psychopharmacology*, vol. 143, pp. 302-8.

Kuepper, R., van Os, J., Lieb, R.M., Wittchen, H.-U., Höfler, M. & Henquet, C. 2011, 'Continued cannabis use and risk of incidence and persistence of psychotic symptoms: 10 year follow-up cohort study', *British Medical Journal*, vol. 342, no. 738, p. 8.

Kumar, R. Chambers, W. & Pertwee, R. 2001, 'Pharmacological actions and therapeutic uses of cannabis and cannabinoids', *Anaesthesia*, vol. 56, no. 11, pp. 1059-68.

Large, M., Sharma, S., Compton, M.T., Slade, T. & Nielssen, O. 2011, 'Cannabis use and earlier onset of psychosis', *Archives of General Psychiatry*, vol. 68, no. 6, 555-61.

Lee, D. & Huestis, M. 2013, 'Current knowledge on cannabinoids in oral fluid', *Drug Testing and Analysis*, vol. 6, pp. 88-111.

Lev-Ran, S., Roerecke, M., Le Foll, B., George, T.P., McKenzie, K. & Rehm, J. 2013, 'The association between cannabis use and depression: A systematic review and meta-analysis of longitudinal studies', *Psychological Medicine*, vol. 44, no. 4, pp. 797-810.

Lynskey, M.T. et al. 2004, 'Major depressive disorder, suicidal ideation, and suicide attempts in twins discordant for cannabis dependence and early-onset cannabis use', *Archives of General Psychiatry*, vol. 61, pp. 1026–32.

Lynskey M.T. et al. 2012, 'An Australian twin study of cannabis and other illicit drug use and misuse, and other psychopathology', *Twin Research and Human Genetics*, vol. 15, pp. 631–41.

Maddux, J.F. & Desmond D.P. 2000, 'Addiction or dependence?' *Addiction*, vol. 95, pp. 661–5.

Maldonado R., Berrendero F., Ozaita, A. & Ronledo, P. 2011, 'Neurochemical basis of cannabis addiction', *Neuroscience*, vol. 181, pp. 1–17.

Margolis, J. 1974, *A Child's Garden of Grass*, Cliff House Books: New York.

Martin, G., Copeland, J., Gates, P. & Gilmour, S. 2006, 'The Severity of Dependence Scale (SDS) in an adolescent population of cannabis users: Reliability, validity and diagnostic cut-off', *Drug and Alcohol Dependence*, vol. 83, pp. 90–3.

Meier M.H. et al. 2012, 'Persistent cannabis users show neuropsychological decline from childhood to midlife', *Proceedings of the National Academy of Sciences*, vol. 109, no. 40, pp. E2657–64.

Menahem, S. 2013, 'Cardiac asystole following cannabis (marijuana) usage—additional mechanism for sudden death?' *Forensic Science International*, vol. 233, pp. e3–e5.

Mittleman M.A. et al. 2001, 'Triggering myocardial infarction by marijuana', *Circulation*, vol. 103, pp. 2805–09.

Mixmag 2014, 'Cannabis madness returns: Debunking tabloid myths', <http://mixmag.net/features/cannabis-madness-returns-debunking-the-latest-myths-about-weed>.

MMWR 2014, 'Youth Risk Behavior Surveillance—United States, 2013', *Morbidity and Mortality Weekly Report*, vol. 63. <http://www.cdc.gov/mmwr/pdf/ss/ss6304.pdf>

Morrison, P. et al. 2009, 'The acute effects of synthetic intravenous Delta9-tetrahydrocannabinol on psychosis, mood and cognitive functioning', *Psychological Medicine*, vol. 39, no. 10, pp. 1607–16.

Norberg, M., MacKenzie, J. & Copeland, J. 2012, 'Quantifying Cannabis Use with the Timeline Followback Approach: A Psychometric Evaluation', *Drug and Alcohol Dependence*, vol. 121, pp. 247–52.

O'Brien C.P., Volkow, N. & Li, T.-K. 2006, 'What's in a word? Addiction versus dependence in DSM-V', *American Journal of Psychiatry*, vol. 163, pp. 764–5.

Panlilio, L.V. et al. 2013, 'Prior exposure to THC increases the addictive effects of nicotine in rats', *Neuropsychopharmacology*, vol. 38, pp. 1198-1209.

Pertwee, R. 2006, 'Cannabinoid pharmacology: the first 66 years', *British Journal of Pharmacology*, vol. 147, pp. S163-S171.

Prochaska, J.O. & DiClemente, C.C. 1982, 'Transtheoretical therapy: Toward a more integrative model of change', *Psychotherapy: Theory, Research and Practice*, vol. 19, pp. 276-88.

Quinn, H.R. et al. 2008, 'Adolescent rats find repeated Δ^9-THC less aversive than adult rats but display greater residual cognitive deficits and changes in hippocampal protein expression following exposure', *Neuropsychopharmacology*, vol. 33, pp. 1113-26.

Ramesh, D., Schlosburg, J.E., Wiebelhaus, J.M. & Lichtman, A.H. 2011, 'Marijuana dependence: Not just smoke and mirrors', *Institute for Laboratory Animal Research*, vol. 52, pp. 295-308.

Ream, G.L., Benoit, E., Johnson, B.D. & Dunlap, E. 2008, 'Smoking tobacco along with marijuana increases symptoms of cannabis dependence', *Drug and Alcohol Dependence*, vol. 95, no. 3, pp. 199-208.

Roffman, R. 2014, *Marijuana Nation*, Pegasus Books, New York.

Rooke, S.E., Copeland, J., Norberg, M.M. et al. 2013, 'Effectiveness of a self-guided web-based cannabis treatment program: Randomized controlled trial', *Journal of Medical Internet Research*, vol. 15, p. e26.

Rooke, S.E., Norberg, M.M. & Copeland, J. 2011, 'Successful and unsuccessful cannabis quitters: Comparing group characteristics and quitting strategies', *Substance Abuse Treatment, Prevention, and Policy*, vol. 6, pp. 30-9.

Rooke, S., Norberg, M., Copeland, J. and Swift, W. 2013. 'Health outcomes associated with long-term regular cannabis and tobacco smoking', *Addictive Behaviors*, vol. 38, pp. 2207-13.

Rosenberg, M.F. & Anthony, J.C. 2001, 'Early clinical manifestations of cannabis dependence in a community sample', *Drug and Alcohol Dependence*, vol. 64, pp. 123-31.

Rubino T., Zamberletti E. & Parolaro, D. 2012, 'Adolescent exposure to cannabis as a risk factor for psychiatric disorders', *Journal of Psychopharmacology*, vol. 26, pp. 177-88.

Sabet, K.A. 2013, *Reefer Sanity: Seven Great Myths About Marijuana*, Beaufort Books, New York.

Spear, L.P. 2013, 'Adolescent neurodevelopment', *Journal of Adolescent Health*, vol. 52, pp. S7-S13.

Substance Abuse and Mental Health Services Administration (SAMHSA) 2013, *Results from the 2012 National Survey on Drug Use and Health: Summary of National Findings*, Substance Abuse and Mental Health Services Administration, Rockville, MD.

Swift, W., Copeland, J. & Hall W. 1998, 'Choosing a diagnostic cut-off for cannabis dependence', *Addiction*, vol. 93, pp. 1681-92.

Swift, W., Hall, W. & Copeland, J. 2000, 'A one-year follow-up of cannabis dependence among long-term cannabis users in Sydney, Australia', *Drug and Alcohol Dependence,* vol. 59, pp. 309-18.

Swift, W., Hall, W. & Teesson, M. 2001, 'Characteristics of DSM-IV and ICD-10 cannabis dependence among Australian adults: Results from the National Survey of Mental Health and Wellbeing', *Drug and Alcohol Dependence*, vol. 63, pp. 147-53.

Swift, W., Wong, A., Li, K.M., Arnold, J.C. & McGregor, I.S. 2013, 'Analysis of cannabis seizures in NSW, Australia: Cannabis potency and cannabinoid profile', *PloS One*, vol. 8, no. 7, p. e70052.

Tashkin D.P. 2013, 'Effects of marijuana smoking on the lung', *Annals of the American Thoracic Society*, vol. 10, no. 3, pp. 239-47.

Tashkin D.P. 1999, 'Effects of cannabis on the respiratory system', in H. Kalant, W. Corrigall, W.D. Hall & R. Smart (eds), *The Health Effects of Cannabis*, Centre for Addictions and Mental Health, Toronto, pp. 311-45.

Thomas, H. 1996, 'Psychiatric symptoms in cannabis users', *Drug & Alcohol Dependence*, vol. 42, no. 3, pp. 201-7.

Tossman, H., Jonas, B., Tensil, M., Lang, P. & Struber E. 2011, 'A controlled trial of an internet-based intervention program for cannabis users', *Cyberpsychology, Behavior, and Social Networking,* vol. 14, no. 11, pp. 673-9.

United Nations Office on Drugs and Crime (UNODC) 2013, *World Drug Report 2013*, United Nations, New York, <www.unodc.org/unodc/secured/wdr/wdr2013/World_Drug_Report_2013.pdf>.

Van Gundy, K. & Rebellon, C. 2010, 'A life-course perspective on the "Gateway Hypothesis"', *Journal of Health and Social Behavior*, vol. 51, pp. 244-59.

Van Ours, J.C., Williams, J., Fergusson, D., Horwood, L.H. 2012, 'Cannabis use and suicidal ideation', *Journal of Health Economics*, vol. 32, no. 3, pp. 524-37.

Wang, G.S., Roosevelt, G. & Heard, K. 2013, 'Pediatric marijuana exposure in a medical marijuana state', *JAMA Pediatrics*, vol. 167, pp. 630-3.

World Health Organization (WHO) 2010, *International Statistical Classification of Diseases and Related Health Problems*, 10th revision, WHO, Malta.

Yücel M. et al. 2008, 'Regional brain abnormalities associated with long-term heavy cannabis use', *Archives of General Psychiatry*, vol. 6, pp. 694-701.

Zammit, S., Allebeck, P., Andreasson, S., Lundberg, I. & Lewis, G. 2002, 'Self-reported cannabis use as a risk factor for schizophrenia in Swedish conscripts of 1969: Historical cohort study', *British Medical Journal*, vol. 325, no. 7374, pp. 1199-1204.

Zammit, S., Moore TH., Lingford-Hughes, A., Barnes, TR., Jones, PB., Burke M. & Lewis G. 2008, 'Effects of cannabis use on outcomes of psychotic disorders: a systematic review', *British Journal of Psychiatry*, vol. 193, no. 5, pp. 357-3.